BAKE WITH BROOKI

Brooke Bellamy opened the doors to her bakery, Brooki Bakehouse in Brisbane, in 2022. Thanks to her hugely popular day-in-the-life videos that take followers behind the scenes of her baking business, Brooke has become globally recognised and now counts millions of followers on TikTok, Instagram and YouTube. Lines of customers await the opening of the bakery each morning, and Brooke and her team ship her famous cookies and brownies around Australia and across the world.

BAKE WITH BROOKI

BROOKE BELLAMY

For anyone who fears they won't find
true love — it's in the kitchen.

CONTENTS

HOW BROOKE BECAME BROOKI

My journey to becoming a bakery owner was a long one that spanned almost every continent, so buckle up – you're in for a ride!

Before I was baking thousands of cookies a day in my tiny but mighty commercial kitchen, I was travelling the world in search of the world's best bakeries. I had taken a gap year after university to find out what I was passionate about and it soon became apparent that my passion lay in seeing the world and eating it. Luckily for me, the two go hand-in-hand.

What was meant to be a gap year soon turned into two years, three, four and eventually an entire decade. To extend my travels and forgo my seemingly inevitable launch into a corporate career, I built myself a website, called myself a travel writer, and somehow spent the entirety of my twenties travelling the world writing for various publications and keeping a journal of my adventures on a travel blog. To say I fell into travel writing would be an accurate description. I saw my writing career as more of a means to an end – the end of which was to see as much of the world as my savings would allow.

Soon into my travels, I realised that I loved discovering food as much as the destination I was visiting. And, more specifically, I loved sweet food. With the trials and tribulations of adulthood pushing me towards a so-called 'real job', growing up baking in the kitchen with my mum now felt like a distant memory. To keep the dream alive, I booked myself patisserie classes in Paris, where I learned to make macarons with a view of the Seine River. Over in North America I walked everywhere

Uptown, Downtown and across town to Brooklyn to find the best cookies in New York City (spoiler: you'll find them at Levain). I visited chocolate factories in Switzerland and scoured the outskirts of Copenhagen in the dark of winter for cardamom buns. Travel soon became the backdrop for my real love affair: baking.

As a new decade approached, I suppose it was only natural I would put my love for sweets into something tangible, so I opened a bakery of my own. I had absolutely no idea what I was doing, naively fumbling through the processes of organising building permits, my first commercial lease, and arranging floorplans and pricing models. It was scary almost all of the time and became only more difficult when the doors opened. My biggest fear was opening to the sound of crickets; in reality, there was a line out the door and up the street! It was equally the most exhilarating and nerve-wracking moment of my life because I realised all too quickly there was no blueprint for running a business. You kind of just have to make it up as you go.

Over the next few years I learned almost everything I know today about baking, operating a business, managing a team, marketing, sales, profit and loss. I could write an entire book on the nitty gritty of owning a business – it really is the hardest thing I have ever done in my life. There's no glamorous way to say you haven't slept more than five hours in the past three months, but somehow you make it through. I hired more help, I even hired my mum. And eventually I would go on to hand her the keys to my business as I packed my bags and ventured off into the world again, in search of something I still hadn't found.

In May of 2022, I opened the doors to Brooki Bakehouse. To say it was an overnight success would be inaccurate, but it certainly was a rapid rise. The first few months were slow and steady as I eased back into the groove of being a business owner/operator. In a single day I would juggle my time between piping macarons and shuffling cookies in and out of the oven. I'd bounce around from the kitchen to the coffee machine, chatting with customers and recommending my new flavour creations. It felt busy because I was wearing so many hats every single day. Little did I know the days of operating my business all on my own would soon be behind me. We had visitors from Sweden, Germany, Singapore, the United States, Brazil and everywhere in between. The moment I realised the line was not a one-off didn't come until a few months later, when I understood that this was our new normal. It seemed word had officially got out that Brooki was where you would find the best cookies in town, and so followed the crowds of customers!

But the real success doesn't come in sales targets, profit margins or new product releases (though these certainly help pay the rent!). Success for me lies in the ability to wake up and do something I truly love. Like really, really *love*. It is by choice I set my alarm each night to arrive at the bakery by 5 am day after day – and stay for longer than twelve hours. With a growing team, we are continuing to push limits and reach milestones week in, week out. And that is perhaps the most exciting part of all: growing a business beyond yourself. We are not only able to offer a place of employment but a place of inspiration, ideas and experimentation. We create flavour ideas and new product development in a WhatsApp group dedicated to the bakery and, now more than ever, I really feel like my love for baking has found meaning.

Through sharing my 'day in the life of a bakery owner' videos I have been able to connect with so many aspiring bakers the world over, and now I am thrilled to share my recipes so you can re-create the magic at home.

Brooki

A DAY IN MY LIFE AS A BAKERY OWNER

Come spend the day with me for a day in my life as a bakery owner!

4.30 a.m. Wake up and immediately make my way to the coffee machine at home. Say good morning to my dog, Frankie, and wait impatiently for my caffeine hit to brew.

4.35 a.m. Get ready for work with a quick routine that consists mostly of brushing my hair tightly into place, often using a wax stick to hold every hair in place in a ballerina-style bun.

4.45 a.m. Delve into my emails as the first order of business. I wish I could say my days start off in a more exciting manner, but I know if I don't attend to my emails first thing in the morning, people will be waiting until the end of the business day to hear back from me. Once you step inside the kitchen it can feel like a bit of a time warp, so I almost always make time to check and respond to emails before leaving the house.

5.45 a.m. Arrive at the bakery and turn on the coffee machine, lights, ovens (in that order), and get ready for my first bake.

6.00 a.m. Prepare at least 60 trays of cookies ready for the oven. Typically, once I have ten trays of cookies ready, the ovens will beep right on cue, indicating they are at the correct temperature. We have two five-tray ovens at Brooki Bakehouse that aren't turned off until late in the afternoon, so it is a never-ending juggle to lay out cookie dough balls on the trays, and trays in the oven, in order to keep up with demand.

6.30 a.m. Sneak in five minutes to prepare myself a second coffee, if I haven't already. Even though I am multitasking between trays of cookies going in and coming out of the oven, the song (of the ovens beeping) and dance (of placing the cookie dough balls perfectly on the tray) is like muscle memory for me. I find this time in the morning oddly therapeutic, before customers arrive and the rest of the team are navigating one another in our small 41-square-metre space.

7.00 a.m. By now, a line has usually started to form outside of the shop. Almost certainly this will be the case on Saturdays, whereas on weekdays it can take a little longer for customers to start lining up. The earliest I have seen a customer wait in line is 5.00 a.m. and the funniest sight I have seen in the line is customers on camping chairs (on more than three occasions). All power to them for the commitment!

7.00 a.m. The rest of the team arrives to set up the pastry case with our range of sweets for the day, garnish cookies, restock packaging and prepare the store for opening.

8.00 a.m. It's show time! The rush of the first hour or two is always a whirlwind, as trying to keep up with demand and ensuring we always have between eight and twelve flavours of cookies in the case at all times is a challenge. We also sell a range of cupcakes, brownies, macarons and ready-made cakes daily, plus coffees and hot chocolates, and let's not forget pre-orders by customers who have arranged to pick up their orders in person.

The rest of the day perhaps unsurprisingly passes in what I can only describe as a blur. There have been countless days where I don't look at the clock once, only noticing how late it is as the sun starts blinding me through the front window, which signifies it is late afternoon.

There was a time when I would regularly find myself in the bakery fifteen hours a day, six days a week. No part of my body or soul misses those long days struggling to stay on two feet, but without the first year of committing myself wholeheartedly to getting the business off the ground, I wouldn't be writing these very words today! I am so grateful to now have a team of bakers, servers and baristas who work alongside me to allow me to work a regular ten-hour shift and I'm glad to say that these days, I even take my five-minute lunch sitting down (on a milk crate of course, in true bakery style!).

TOOLS OF THE TRADE

Successfully following a recipe is much easier when you're equipped with the right tools. Back in the early years of baking in my home kitchen, before I opened the bakery, I learned the hard way how much simpler life is when you set yourself up for success. These are the essential tools I recommend all bakers have in their kitchen – and, indeed, all the ones you will need to bake this book from start to finish.

STAND MIXER

A stand mixer is the workhorse of the kitchen and although it is one of the more expensive investments you'll make as a baker, it is certainly the one that will pay off most. My first stand mixer was a 4.8-litre (5.5-qt) cream-coloured KitchenAid and I still use it in my home kitchen to this day. If you have the budget to opt for a slightly larger size, I have found the 6.6-litre (7-qt) KitchenAid mixer to be more user-friendly and versatile, as I am often baking large enough batches to share around with friends and family.

KITCHEN SCALES

Bakers and pastry chefs measure almost everything in grams, with a set of scales at the ready. Using scales is a guaranteed way to ensure your success in the kitchen, as it must be said that baking is science – chemistry, if you will – and using precise measurements is the single best way to get the right result from a recipe. I give metric and imperial in my recipes, and for my notes on weights, measures and conversions, refer to page 310.

SUGAR THERMOMETER

I never really understood the need for a sugar thermometer until I started making macarons. I suppose this was because I didn't grow up using one to bake my basic recipes, so it seemed like a foreign entity to me in the kitchen – intimidating, even. For any baker who wishes to progress to macarons, toffees and candies, becoming familiar with a sugar thermometer is essential. You'll see how simple it is to use one when we reach the macarons chapter, but for now, invest in a good-quality one from the kitchen store.

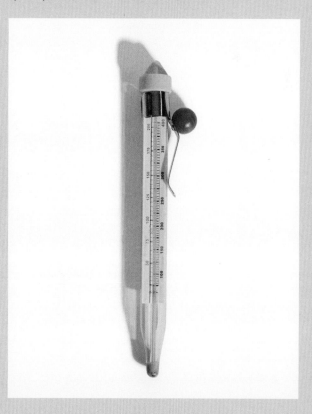

CAKE TURNTABLE

If you dream of becoming great at decorating cakes, be sure to invest in a good-quality cake turntable. With the help of a cake turntable, you can cut, stack, crumb coat and ice cakes in a fraction of the time it would take without one. Opt for one that is sturdy enough to hold the weight of a cake, wide enough for the diameter of the cakes you plan to make, and spins with ease.

MIXING BOWLS

Every baker needs at least a few mixing bowls in various sizes. Not only are they great for combining dry ingredients before they are placed in the mixer, but they're also handy when it comes to measuring ingredients for *mise en place* (a fancy French term for getting everything weighed and 'in its place' before you start baking).

FINE MESH SIEVE

There are often ingredients that call for sifting; however, in this book I will only call for sifting where it is absolutely essential. I don't know of many bakers – professional or in their home kitchen – who prefer to add an extra step to the recipe where it is not required. Sifting ingredients is not always necessary, but in times where it is, a fine mesh sieve comes in handy.

BAKING TINS AND TRAYS

What would a baker be without tins and trays? Hungry! I recommend having two baking trays, two 20 cm (8") round cake tins, two 12-cup cupcake baking pans and a wire cooling rack or two.

SPATULAS

If there's one tool in the kitchen I can never have enough of, it is spatulas. In the bakery I probably have at least twenty spatulas in my section alone and somehow that still never seems like enough. Perfect for scraping the bowl, mixing ingredients, lifting cookies off the tray – you name it, I use a spatula for it.

OFFSET SPATULA

Another necessity in the cake realm, offset spatulas make distributing filling between layers easy, and are the most efficient way to quickly spread the top and sides of your cake with buttercream or chocolate ganache.

CAKE SCRAPER

Once your cakes are stacked, you'll need a tool that effortlessly scrapes away the excess buttercream. Enter: the cake scraper. These handy little numbers make icing cakes a whole lot easier and come in a range of sizes. My favourite size is 23 cm tall, as I find it the most adaptable for the majority of cakes we make in the bakery.

DOUGH SCRAPER

Different in both name and shape to the aforementioned cake scraper, a dough scraper has a rounded edge, perfect for scraping the sides of your mixing bowl. In the Brooki kitchen we call the dough scraper the 'money maker', as it quite literally scrapes the money (ingredients) from the bowl, leaving no waste.

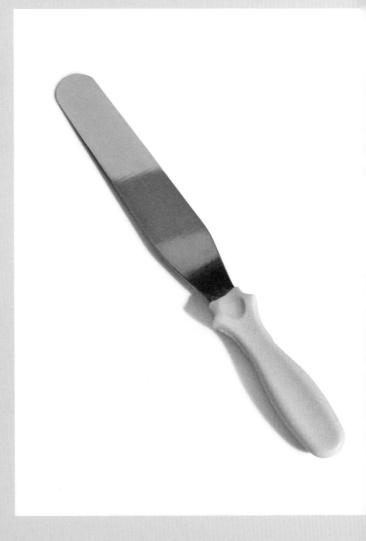

ICE-CREAM SCOOP

Don't let the name fool you – there's no ice-cream making in this book (I quite frankly have never dabbled in making it, though I do possess an undying love for consuming it). No, instead we will be using an ice-cream scoop to portion our cupcake batter into the pans. It's the quickest way to achieve perfectly portioned cupcakes without spilling batter everywhere.

PIPING BAG AND TIPS

Piping bags are used in so many of the recipes in this book and, indeed, I use my fair share in the bakery daily. The trick is to find good-quality piping bags that will remain intact no matter how thick the batter you're piping. Reusable piping bags are a great long-term alternative to single-use piping bags; however, there are some wonderful biodegradable disposable bags on the market now for conscious consumers. Piping tips come in many different shapes and sizes, however there are a few iconic piping tips I think every baker should have in their collection.

2A: One of the most versatile, this is a large round piping tip, perfect for piping macaron shells, or for smoothly piping buttercream on top of cupcakes.

Wilton 8B: One of my favourite piping tips for cupcakes. This open star tip is easy to use and great for piping buttercream.

Wilton 1M: Also known as a rose piping tip. It's an elegant choice, perfect for piping rosettes on cakes, or a rose shaped buttercream swirl on top of your freshly baked cupcake bases.

BAKING PAPER

Baking paper or parchment paper, as it is often referred to, is a baker's best friend. Over the years, baking pans have professed to be everything from non-stick to rose gold, but none of the glitz and glamour will ever replace good old-fashioned baking paper. Whether you're lining a cake tin or baking a tray of chunky cookies, baking paper is essential for almost any recipe in this book and can be found at your local supermarket. My preferred method of greasing cake tins is with cooking spray, as it is a quick and easy way to help line your pans that almost always guarantees your bakes pop out immediately once they have cooled.

SILICONE MATS

Non-stick silicone baking mats have been used in commercial kitchens for years, but have only recently become popular in home kitchens. Useful for a variety of baked goods, they're perfect for meringues and macarons, not least because they have a convenient circle template printed on them so you know where and how much mixture to pipe to give you macarons of equal size every time. They're worth the splurge if you plan to use them for years to come and are a great reusable alternative to baking paper where the recipe allows.

STAPLE INGREDIENTS

Baking has always been my favourite pastime on a Sunday afternoon, so I make sure to do my grocery run on a Saturday morning. There are, however, some staple baking ingredients that it's good to always have on hand.

UNSALTED BUTTER

High-fat butter is an essential ingredient when aiming for topnotch baked goods. The higher the fat content, the lower the water content (82 per cent butterfat or higher is considered high-fat). If flavour matters to you, the percentage of fat should too. As for salted or unsalted, I always use unsalted butter in baking to have full control over the salt levels in a recipe. All recipes in this book call for unsalted butter.

EGGS

Eggs are another essential in baking and when it comes to high quality, free-range eggs will always be preferred. All of the recipes in this book call for large (50 g), room-temperature eggs (see page 13 for why). But if you've left it to the last minute and your eggs are cold, fear not! A quick hack to bring eggs to room temperature quickly is to sit them, still in their shell, in a bowl of warm tap water for 5 minutes. Dry them off before using, et voila!

HIGH-QUALITY CHOCOLATE

Chocolate is one of the ingredients where quality really matters. That doesn't mean it has to be outrageously expensive or hard to find – you can source high-quality chocolate from the supermarket. Brands like Lindt and Whittaker's offer delicious supermarket chocolate; just be sure to reach for 70 per cent. Alternatively, if you're in the commercial space, Callebaut, Belcolade and Veliche are my favourite Belgian chocolatiers with ethical cocoa sourcing.

DUTCH COCOA POWDER

On the subject of chocolate, there is no substitute for Dutch cocoa powder – facts! Growing up, I was not aware there was a better quality cocoa powder out there than regular supermarket cocoa, but believe me when I say there is – and it matters. Dutch cocoa powder (also known as alkalised cocoa powder because its acidity has been removed) is the only cocoa powder we use in the bakery, and the same goes for my home kitchen. With a higher cocoa fat content, Dutch cocoa powder gives your bakes a richer, smoother and more intensely chocolatey flavour, so it is well worth the investment.

BROWN SUGAR

Brown sugar has different names and meanings depending on whereabouts in the world you're from. The brown sugar referred to in this cookbook is fine and moist, also known as light brown sugar. Brown sugar has a higher molasses count for that delicious caramel flavour, making it the perfect ingredient to give your bakes a well-rounded flavour profile.

CREAM CHEESE

As you will come to learn throughout this book, I *really* love cream cheese. Whether it be whipped in a cream cheese frosting atop

my Red Velvet Cupcakes or the foundational ingredient of a silky-smooth cheesecake, there is nothing that gets me excited about biting into a fresh bake more than knowing the recipe includes cream cheese. As always in baking, full-fat dairy is the way to go. Light versions have a higher water content that sacrifices flavour, so be sure to keep this in mind when baking for the best possible taste! I prefer Philadelphia cream cheese above all others.

VANILLA
You will notice that vanilla is widely used in this book. Vanilla adds an aroma to your baked goods and allows the flavours to really shine. Not all vanillas are the same – you have vanilla bean paste, vanilla extract and vanilla essence (synthetic). I believe the real stuff always tastes better than the knock-off, so I choose to use vanilla extract in my recipes. You can of course substitute with vanilla bean for a more intense flavour, or vanilla essence for a more affordable alternative.

FOOD COLOURING
Quite a few of the recipes in this book call for food colouring, and rightfully so – after all, baking should be fun, vibrant and full of colour. Where natural colours are not present, I like to give my creations a pop of colour if it makes sense. But when it comes to food colouring, no two types are the same. Gel food colouring is best used for recipes going in the oven (like cupcakes or macarons), whereas oil-based colours are better for colouring buttercream. As for brands, I mostly use AmeriColor gels for oven-baked goods. Colour Mill, which is the only brand I use to colour our buttercream in the bakery, is my go-to oil-based colour.

FULL-FAT DAIRY
Using light alternatives for milk, sour cream or cream has very little benefit in terms of calories, but it has detrimental effects in terms of the final taste of a baked product. For the best results, I highly recommend using only full-fat dairy products.

PLAIN FLOUR VS. SELF-RAISING FLOUR
A lot of the recipes in this book use a mix of plain flour and self-raising flour. If you can't get a hold of self-raising flour where you live, it is pretty easy to substitute plain flour. Self-raising flour is essentially plain flour mixed with the addition of raising agent, so follow the instructions below if you ever need to make your own.

How to turn plain flour into self-raising flour

To every 200 g (7 oz) of plain flour add 10 g (2 teaspoons) of baking powder and mix with a whisk to distribute it evenly through the flour.

MY BEST BAKING TIPS

I have purposefully avoided naming these 'baking rules', but rather my best tips for baking success. These are general tips that I believe will make you a better baker almost instantly.

READ THE RECIPE

You've heard it before but I'll say it again for good measure: read the recipe in full before you begin baking. Sometimes a recipe will require preparation a day ahead, which is not helpful to discover halfway through if you're pressed for time.

GET PREPARED – *MISE EN PLACE*

Mise en place is a French term for getting set up, used to refer to measuring out your ingredients before beginning and ensuring you have all the tools required for the recipe out on the bench and ready to go. Think of your home kitchen a bit like a cooking show, with everything within arm's reach before you start baking. You will be surprised at how much easier it is to bake this way!

TASTE AS YOU GO

As you continue on your baking journey, you will soon realise that many recipes are similar, with slight tweaks from the chef here and there to add their spin to suit their taste. The fun part about baking comes when you realise you can make your own adjustments, experimenting over time as you become more familiar with a recipe. Tasting as you go is the best way to start tweaking recipes to your own liking – you might want to add a sprinkle of salt to a biscuit crumb,

for example, or a tablespoon of honey for some natural sweetness.

KNOW WHEN TO EXPERIMENT

That said, it is important to know when to experiment and when to follow the recipe. The last thing you want is a cookie that is dry or tastes of baking soda, so be sure to limit experimenting to taste, rather than rushing to change the base science of a recipe!

ROOM-TEMPERATURE INGREDIENTS

As you will come to see in this book, most recipes call for room-temperature butter, eggs, cream cheese, buttermilk, etc. Be sure to take note of these instructions as it is important for the science of the recipe to shine through. By way of example, room-temperature eggs mix more easily in a cake batter, allowing them to combine into the batter quickly. If using cold eggs, you need to increase the mix time, which incorporates unnecessary air into the batter and prevents the ingredients from emulsifying properly.

GET TO KNOW YOUR OVEN

The recipes in this book are geared towards fan-forced ovens. If using a convection oven, increase the temperature by 25°C (45°F). As a general disclaimer, no two ovens are the same. The temperatures given here are a general guideline and will suit most fan-forced ovens. However, it is important to note that every oven will have hot patches – areas of the oven that heat more quickly than others. Over time, you will learn where these are in your oven and potentially rotate your bakes during the baking process. Just be sure to never open the oven until you're at least halfway through the baking time, if rotating your trays.

ALWAYS SCRAPE THE BOWL

I don't know where I'd be without my stand mixer – probably in a great deal of pain! The benefit of using a stand mixer is that you will significantly cut down the time and labour that goes into hand mixing all of your baked goods. But the reality is, you will still need to scrape down the sides of the bowl as you mix, to ensure no ingredients get stuck to the sides of the bowl (butter being the key offender).

DON'T OVER MIX YOUR CAKE BATTER

You will often see the phrase 'mix until just combined' in a baking recipe, or 'be careful not to over mix'. This is usually in reference to the moment you combine wet and dry ingredients. Over mixing a batter can lead to excess development of gluten, which is the structural protein found in wheat flours. This will typically result in a deflated or dense cake, rather than a deliciously fluffy sponge.

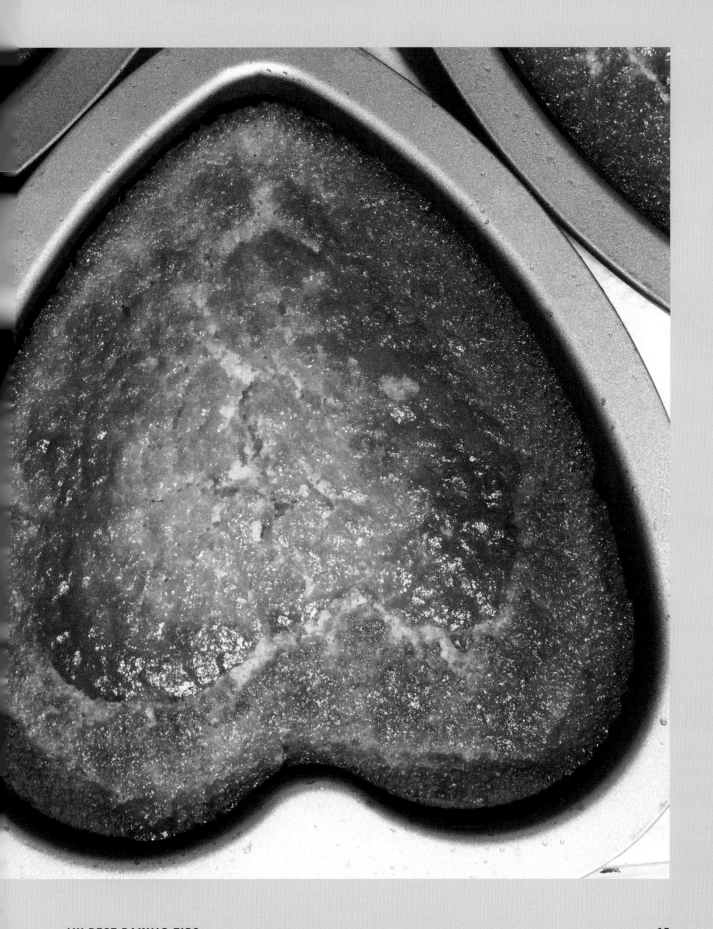

COOKIES

It feels only natural to start with cookies, since they're the single reason my bakery found success. In the bakery, our cookies are chunky, oversized, bursting with flavour and quite often packed with gooey goodness. It was back in New York City in my early twenties when I first discovered the chunky New York style of cookie at the original Levain Bakery on 74th Street. I wasn't a cookie connoisseur at the time, perhaps even a little apprehensive about taking the subway so far uptown just for a cookie. That all changed when, right there on the sidewalk of the Upper West Side, I had an epiphany. These cookies are seriously *that good*, I thought to myself. What ensued was nothing short of an obsession with creating my own version of these cookies. After endless iterations and recipe adaptations, I finally landed on the perfect cookie recipe. And now I'm passing it on to you. You're welcome!

RED VELVET

NYC

CHOC CHIP

BISCOFF

NUTELLA BUENO

TRIPLE CHOC

New York Cookies

If you've turned to this page before reading anything else in this recipe book, I don't blame you! If there's one cookie recipe that made my bakery famous, it is this one – and there's a good reason why: it is hands-down the best cookie recipe on the planet. While not everyone loves nuts, be sure to try this recipe with the inclusion of walnuts, as they really produce the perfect taste and texture profile of this classic chunky cookie. And if you're wondering what makes this cookie so delicious, it's the harmonious blend of flavours thanks to the dark chocolate chips, the texture thanks to the walnuts, and the fact that every bite is characterised by a crispy exterior with a soft centre that melts in your mouth.

MAKES: 8–10 LARGE COOKIES
PREPARATION TIME: 15 MINUTES
COOKING TIME: 16–18 MINUTES
COOLING TIME: 10–15 MINUTES

185 g (6½ oz) unsalted butter, cubed and cold
130 g (4½ oz) caster sugar
130 g (4½ oz) light brown sugar
2 large eggs, room temperature
160 g (5½ oz) self-raising flour
240 g (8½ oz) plain flour
¼ teaspoon of bicarbonate of soda
1½ teaspoon of baking powder
pinch of salt
320 g (11¼ oz) dark chocolate chips
80 g (2¾ oz) walnuts, roughly chopped

In the bowl of a stand mixer with the paddle attachment, beat the butter for 2 minutes on medium speed. Add the sugars and beat for a further 2–3 minutes. Scrape down the sides of the bowl to ensure all of the butter is fully incorporated.

Add the eggs one at a time on low speed until just incorporated.

Add the dry ingredients and beat until fully incorporated.

On low speed, add the chocolate chips and walnuts.

Weigh each cookie dough ball to 150 g (5¼ oz). Chill in the fridge for at least 3 hours before baking.

When ready to bake, preheat the oven to 180°C (400°F) and line a baking tray with baking paper. Place cookie dough balls onto the tray at least 2 cm (¾") apart and bake for 16–18 minutes until golden on top.

Allow to cool for 10–15 minutes before enjoying. (Try not to be impatient; the cookies need this time to continue cooking at room temperature!)

STORAGE
Once baked, these cookies will last for 5–7 days in an airtight container at room temperature. Alternatively, you can freeze raw dough balls for up to 3 months and bake for a few more minutes from frozen.

CUSTOMISATIONS
If you fancy smaller cookies, weigh the dough balls at 50 g (1¾ oz) per cookie. Bake for 10–12 minutes at the same temperature.

If you have a nut allergy or prefer your cookies sans nuts, you can choose to omit the walnuts in this recipe. Nuts do, however, add that bit of extra crunch and nutty richness, so results may vary.

Red Velvet Cookies

While New York Cookies are my bakery's bestseller, Red Velvet come a very close second. At times, this type will outsell every other variety of cookie in the bakery. It has become a bit of a sport for local office workers to visit at various times of the day to see if they can grab one to woo their colleagues. The truth is, these cookies are mind-blowingly awesome. There really is no other way to say it. If you love a creamy, rich flavour matched with a meltingly soft texture, this cookie has your name on it.

MAKES: 8 LARGE COOKIES
PREPARATION TIME: 15 MINUTES
COOKING TIME: 16–18 MINUTES
COOLING TIME: 10–15 MINUTES

160 g (5½ oz) cream cheese frosting (see page 287)
300 g (10½ oz) plain flour
1 tablespoon of Dutch cocoa powder
1 teaspoon of baking powder
½ teaspoon of bicarbonate of soda
pinch of salt
125 g (4½ oz) unsalted butter, room temperature
150 g (5¼ oz) caster sugar
100 g (3½ oz) light brown sugar
1 large egg, room temperature
1 teaspoon of vanilla extract
1 teaspoon of red food colouring
300 g (10½ oz) white chocolate chips

Scoop 20 g (¾ oz) balls of cream cheese frosting onto a lined baking tray and place in the freezer to set. Meanwhile, prepare the cookie dough.

Place the flour, cocoa powder, baking powder, bicarbonate of soda and salt in a bowl and mix to combine. Set aside.

In the bowl of a stand mixer with the paddle attachment, beat the butter for 2 minutes on medium speed. Add the sugars and beat for a further 3–5 minutes. Scrape down the sides of the bowl to ensure all of the butter is fully incorporated.

Add the egg, vanilla and red food colouring on low speed until just incorporated.

Add the dry ingredients and beat until fully incorporated.

On low speed, add the chocolate chips to combine.

Weigh each cookie dough ball to 130 g (4½ oz). Once all the balls are weighed, create a bird's nest shape in each ball and place a ball of cream cheese frosting inside. Carefully wrap the dough around the cream cheese until the dough completely covers it. Chill in the fridge for at least 3 hours before baking.

When ready to bake, preheat the oven to 180°C (400°F) and line a baking tray with baking paper. Place cookie dough balls onto the tray at least 2 cm (¾") apart and bake for 16–18 minutes until golden on top.

Allow to cool for 10–15 minutes before enjoying. (Try not to be impatient; the cookies need this time to continue cooking at room temperature!)

STORAGE
These cookies have a shorter shelf life due to their cream cheese filling. Store in the fridge for up to 3 days in an airtight container. If you prefer not to bake them all at once, freeze filled raw dough balls in an airtight container on the day they are made, for up to 1 month, and bake for a few more minutes from frozen.

Classic Choc Chip Cookies

Every baker has a classic choc chip cookie in their repertoire, and this is mine. When I was younger, I favoured the sweetness of milk chocolate chips, but with age – and I can't believe I'm saying this – I have grown more fond of dark chocolate chips in my cookies. This recipe calls for both in an effort to sit on the fence and find the perfect balance, but you can just as easily use all milk chocolate chips for a sweeter cookie, or all dark chocolate chips for a richer bittersweetness.

MAKES: 8 LARGE COOKIES
PREPARATION TIME: 10 MINUTES
COOKING TIME: 16–18 MINUTES
COOLING TIME: 10–15 MINUTES

200 g (7 oz) unsalted butter, room temperature
180 g (6¼ oz) light brown sugar
80 g (2¾ oz) caster sugar
1 large egg, room temperature
250 g (9 oz) self-raising flour
200 g (7 oz) plain flour
pinch of salt
1 teaspoon of baking powder
150 g (5¼ oz) dark chocolate chips
150 g (5¼ oz) milk chocolate chips

In the bowl of a stand mixer with the paddle attachment, beat the butter for 2 minutes on medium speed. Add the sugars and beat for a further 3–5 minutes. Scrape down the sides of the bowl to ensure all of the butter is fully incorporated.

Add the egg and beat on low speed until just incorporated.

Add the dry ingredients and beat on low speed until just incorporated.

On low speed, add the chocolate chips to combine.

Weigh each cookie dough ball to 150 g (5¼ oz). Chill in the fridge for at least 3 hours before baking.

When ready to bake, preheat the oven to 180°C (400°F) and line a baking tray with baking paper. Place cookie dough balls onto the tray at least 2 cm (¾") apart and bake for 16–18 minutes until golden on top.

Allow to cool for 10–15 minutes before enjoying. (Try not to be impatient; the cookies need this time to continue cooking at room temperature!)

STORAGE
Once baked, these cookies will last for 5–7 days in an airtight container at room temperature. Alternatively, you can freeze raw dough balls for up to 3 months and bake for a few more minutes from frozen.

Triple Choc Cookies

These cookies are not for the faint-hearted. At the risk of stating the obvious, you'll need to love chocolate to truly love these cookies and savour every bite. Best served warm out of the oven with a generous scoop of ice-cream and Hot Chocolate Fudge Sauce, these cookies will cure your chocolate cravings in just one bite.

MAKES: 8 LARGE COOKIES
PREPARATION TIME: 10 MINUTES
COOKING TIME: 16–18 MINUTES
COOLING TIME: 10–15 MINUTES

190 g (6¾ oz) unsalted butter, room temperature
290 g (10¼ oz) caster sugar
2 large eggs, room temperature
50 g (1¾ oz) Dutch cocoa powder
270 g (9½ oz) plain flour
1 teaspoon of cornflour
1 teaspoon of bicarbonate of soda
pinch of salt
200 g (7 oz) dark chocolate chips
100 g (3½ oz) milk chocolate chips
vanilla ice-cream and Hot Chocolate Fudge Sauce
  (see page 298), to serve

In the bowl of a stand mixer with the paddle attachment, beat the butter for 2 minutes on medium speed. Add the sugar and beat for a further 2–3 minutes. Scrape down the sides of the bowl to ensure all of the butter is fully incorporated.

Add eggs, one at a time, on low speed until just incorporated.

Add the dry ingredients and beat until fully incorporated.

On low speed, add the chocolate chips and mix to combine.

Weigh each cookie dough ball to 150 g (5¼ oz). Chill in the fridge for at least 3 hours before baking.

When ready to bake, preheat the oven to 180°C (400°F) and line a baking tray with baking paper. Place cookie dough balls onto the tray at least 2 cm (¾") apart and bake for 16–18 minutes until golden on top.

Allow to cool for 10–15 minutes before enjoying. (Try not to be impatient; the cookies need this time to continue cooking at room temperature!)

Serve with vanilla ice-cream and Hot Chocolate Fudge Sauce.

STORAGE
Once baked, these cookies will last for 5–7 days in an airtight container at room temperature. Alternatively, you can freeze raw dough balls for up to 3 months and bake for a few more minutes from frozen.

CUSTOMISATIONS
Customising the chocolate cookie dough base is easy and, for me, the most fun part of the process. Some flavours we like to make in the bakery include choc peanut chip cookies (swap the chocolate chips for Reese's Peanut Butter Baking Chips) and dark chocolate raspberry (keep the dark chocolate chips but substitute the milk chocolate chips for the same quantity of freeze-dried raspberries).

Almond Croissant Cookies

My favourite breakfast pastry has always been an almond croissant. Flaky and crispy on the outside, soft and full of buttery almond cream in the centre. The baked almond flakes give these pastries a depth you don't get in a regular croissant, plus they're just outrageously full of sugar and sometimes all you need is for your breakfast pastry to hit hard. So, why not make it a cookie? I didn't know this cookie would amass a worldwide audience when I first created it, but once you try it for yourself, you will know why it has a cult following!

MAKES: 8–10 COOKIES
PREPARATION TIME: 30 MINUTES
COOKING TIME: 16–18 MINUTES
COOLING TIME: 15–20 MINUTES

For the almond cream filling:
50 g (1¾ oz) white sugar
40 g (1½ oz) almond meal
pinch of salt
55 g (2 oz) unsalted butter, cubed
1 large egg

For the cookie base:
200 g (7 oz) unsalted butter, room temperature
180 g (6¼ oz) light brown sugar
80 g (2¾ oz) caster sugar
1 large egg, room temperature
250 g (9 oz) self-raising flour
200 g (7 oz) plain flour
pinch of salt
1 teaspoon of baking powder
300 g (10½ oz) white chocolate chips

For rolling the dough:
100 g (3½ oz) almond flakes

icing sugar, to serve

To make the almond cream:

Line a baking tray with baking paper.

In the bowl of a stand mixer with the whisk attachment, combine white sugar, almond meal and salt. Mix well on medium-high speed until incorporated.

Next, add the butter and mix well.

Finally, add the egg and mix on medium-high speed for about 2 minutes, until the mixture is light and fluffy.

Scoop the mixture into 20 g (¾ oz) balls, placing them on the prepared baking tray. Place in the freezer to set while you make the cookie dough.

To make the cookie dough:

In the bowl of a stand mixer, beat the butter for 2 minutes on medium speed. Add the sugars and beat for a further 2–3 minutes. Scrape down the sides of the bowl to ensure all of the butter is fully incorporated.

Add the egg on low speed and mix until just combined.

Add the dry ingredients and beat until just combined.

On low speed, add the chocolate chips and mix until just combined.

Weigh each cookie dough ball to 130 g (4½ oz). Once all the dough is measured, mould each dough ball into a bird's nest shape and place a ball of chilled almond cream in the centre. Carefully wrap the cookie dough around the almond cream. Roll each dough ball in the almond flakes and chill in the fridge for at least 3 hours before baking.

STORAGE
These cookies have a shorter shelf life due to the almond cream filling. Store in the fridge for up to 3 days in an airtight container, or freeze raw dough balls for up to 1 month. If freezing, allow cookie dough balls to thaw in the fridge overnight before baking.

When ready to bake, preheat the oven to 180°C (400°F) and line a baking tray with baking paper. Place cookie dough balls onto the tray at least 2 cm (¾") apart and bake for 16–18 minutes until golden on top.

Allow to cool for 10–15 minutes. (Try not to be impatient; the cookies need this time to continue cooking at room temperature!)

Finally, dust with icing sugar before enjoying.

Nutella Bueno Cookies

If there ever was a perfect cookie recipe for Nutella fans, this would be it. The classic dough base is the ideal backdrop for the silky smooth Nutella spread to take centre-stage, while the addition of Kinder Bueno chunks to the milk chocolate chips makes for a creamy, nutty surprise in every bite.

MAKES: 8–10 COOKIES
PREPARATION TIME: 10 MINUTES
COOKING TIME: 16–18 MINUTES
COOLING TIME: 10–15 MINUTES

160 g (5½ oz) Nutella spread
200 g (7 oz) unsalted butter, room temperature
180 g (6¼ oz) light brown sugar
80 g (2¾ oz) caster sugar
1 large egg, room temperature
250 g (9 oz) self-raising flour
200 g (7 oz) plain flour
pinch of salt
1 teaspoon of baking powder
200 g (7 oz) milk chocolate chips
100 g (3½ oz) Kinder Bueno pieces
Kinder Bueno pieces and Nutella, to decorate (optional)

Line a baking tray with baking paper, and scoop the Nutella into 20 g (¾ oz) balls onto it. Place in the freezer to set while you make the cookie dough.

In the bowl of a stand mixer with the paddle attachment, beat the butter for 2 minutes on medium speed. Add the sugars and beat for a further 3–5 minutes. Scrape down the sides of the bowl to ensure all of the butter is fully incorporated.

Add the egg and beat on low speed until just incorporated.

Add the dry ingredients and beat on low speed until just incorporated.

Add the chocolate chips and Bueno pieces, beating to combine. The Bueno pieces should break up.

Weigh each cookie dough ball to 130 g (4½ oz). Once all the dough is measured, mould each dough ball into a bird's nest shape and place a frozen Nutella ball in the centre. Carefully wrap the cookie dough around the Nutella so it is completely covered. Chill the dough balls in the fridge for at least 3 hours before baking.

When ready to bake, preheat the oven to 180°C (400°F) and line a baking tray with baking paper. Place cookie dough balls onto the tray at least 2 cm (¾") apart and bake for 16–18 minutes until golden on top.

Allow to cool for 10–15 minutes before topping each cookie with a piece of Bueno dipped into Nutella to garnish (optional).

STORAGE
Once baked, these cookies will last for 5–7 days in an airtight container at room temperature. Alternatively, you can freeze raw dough balls for up to 3 months and bake for a few more minutes from frozen.

Biscoff Cookies

Every time a customer asks me to explain the flavour of Biscoff, I come up short. There just aren't enough words in the English language to describe the caramelised biscuit taste that is Biscoff, with its subtle hints of cinnamon, nutmeg and ginger.

This particular cookie has been described by one of our bakers as the only time she has ever enjoyed anything Biscoff – and she now goes on to buy a Biscoff Cookie at the end of every shift.

MAKES: 8–10 COOKIES
PREPARATION TIME: 10 MINUTES
COOKING TIME: 16–18 MINUTES
COOLING TIME: 10–15 MINUTES

160 g (5½ oz) Biscoff spread
200 g (7 oz) unsalted butter, room temperature
180 g (6¼ oz) light brown sugar
80 g (2¾ oz) caster sugar
1 large egg, room temperature
250 g (9 oz) self-raising flour
200 g (7 oz) plain flour
pinch of salt
1 teaspoon of baking powder
200 g (7 oz) white chocolate chips
100 g (3½ oz) Biscoff biscuits, roughly chopped

10 Biscoff biscuits and Biscoff spread,
 to decorate (optional)

Line a baking tray with baking paper and scoop the Biscoff into 20 g (¾ oz) balls onto it. Place in the freezer to set while you make the cookie dough.

In the bowl of a stand mixer with the paddle attachment, beat the butter for 2 minutes on medium speed. Add the sugars and beat for a further 3–5 minutes. Scrape down the sides of the bowl to ensure all of the butter is fully incorporated.

Add the egg and beat on low speed until just incorporated.

Add the dry ingredients and beat on low speed until just incorporated.

Add the chocolate chips and Biscoff biscuit pieces, beating to combine.

Weigh each cookie dough ball to 130 g (4½ oz). Once all the dough is measured, mould each dough ball into a bird's nest shape and place a frozen Biscoff ball in the centre. Carefully wrap the cookie dough around the Biscoff so it is completely covered. Chill the dough balls in the fridge for at least 3 hours before baking.

When ready to bake, preheat the oven to 180°C (400°F) and line a baking tray with baking paper. Place cookie dough balls onto the tray at least 2 cm (¾") apart and bake for 16–18 minutes until golden on top.

Allow to cool for 10–15 minutes before enjoying. (Try not to be impatient; the cookies need this time to continue cooking at room temperature!)

When completely cool, stick a Biscoff biscuit onto each cookie with a small blob of Biscoff spread, to decorate (optional).

STORAGE
Once baked, these cookies will last for 5–7 days in an airtight container at room temperature. Alternatively, you can freeze raw dough balls for up to 3 months and bake for a few more minutes from frozen.

Ferrero Rocher Fudge Cookies

Sometimes, you just crave something rich, decadent and disgustingly chocolatey. Please make way for this Ferrero Rocher Fudge Cookie to enter the chat. Complete with a chocolate base cookie dough wrapped around a Ferrero Rocher dipped in Nutella, this is the kind of cookie where it might not only be possible but necessary to stop after your first one.

MAKES: 8–10 COOKIES
PREPARATION TIME: 15 MINUTES
COOKING TIME: 16–18 MINUTES
COOLING TIME: 10–15 MINUTES

190 g (6¾ oz) unsalted butter, room temperature
290 g (10¼ oz) caster sugar
1 teaspoon of vanilla extract
2 large eggs, room temperature
50 g (1¾ oz) Dutch cocoa powder
270 g (9½ oz) plain flour
1 teaspoon of cornflour
1 teaspoon of bicarbonate of soda
pinch of salt
300 g (10½ oz) milk chocolate chips
100 g (3½ oz) chopped hazelnuts (optional)
10 Ferrero Rochers
Nutella

10 Ferrero Rochers and Nutella, to decorate
 (optional)

In the bowl of a stand mixer with the paddle attachment, beat the butter for 2 minutes on medium speed. Add the sugar and beat for a further 2–3 minutes. Scrape down the sides of the bowl to ensure all of the butter is fully incorporated.

Add vanilla and eggs, one at a time, on low speed until just incorporated.

Add the dry ingredients and beat until fully incorporated.

On low speed, add the chocolate chips and mix until just incorporated.

Weigh each cookie dough ball to 100 g (3½ oz). Mould each cookie dough ball into the shape of a bird's nest. Dip a Ferrero Rocher into the Nutella before placing in the centre of the dough ball. Carefully wrap the cookie dough around the Ferrero Rocher until completely covered in cookie dough. Chill in the fridge for at least 3 hours before baking.

When ready to bake, preheat the oven to 180°C (400°F) and line a baking tray with baking paper. Place cookie dough balls onto the tray at least 2 cm (¾") apart and bake for 16–18 minutes until golden on top.

Allow to cool for 10–15 minutes before enjoying. (Try not to be impatient; the cookies need this time to continue cooking at room temperature!)

When completely cool, stick a Ferrero Rocher onto each cookie with a small blob of Nutella, to decorate (optional).

STORAGE
Once baked, these cookies will last for 5–7 days in an airtight container at room temperature. Alternatively, you can freeze raw dough balls for up to 3 months and bake for a few more minutes from frozen.

Salted Caramel Cookies

There's a special place in my heart for salted caramel flavoured anything. It was a love affair that started back in Paris on my first solo trip to the French capital, where I discovered the magic that occurs when you add a happy dose of salt to a batch of caramel (this was almost a rite of passage into adulthood during the 2000s, when salted caramel swept the world). Nowadays almost everyone loves salted caramel, making this the perfect cookie to make for a special event and win over the guest list in just one bite.

MAKES: 8–10 LARGE COOKIES
PREPARATION TIME: 10 MINUTES
COOKING TIME: 16–18 MINUTES
COOLING TIME: 10–15 MINUTES

160 g (5½ oz) Salted Caramel Sauce, chilled (page 300)
200 g (7 oz) unsalted butter, room temperature
180 g (6¼ oz) light brown sugar
80 g (2¾ oz) caster sugar
1 large egg, room temperature
250 g (9 oz) self-raising flour
200 g (7 oz) plain flour
pinch of salt
1 teaspoon of baking powder
200 g (7 oz) white chocolate chips

sea salt flakes, to garnish

Line a baking tray with baking paper and scoop the chilled Salted Caramel Sauce into 20 g (¾ oz) balls onto it. Place in the freezer to set while you make the cookie dough.

In the bowl of a stand mixer with the paddle attachment, beat the butter for 2 minutes on medium speed. Add the sugars and beat for a further 3–5 minutes. Scrape down the sides of the bowl to ensure all of the butter is fully incorporated.

Add the egg and beat on low speed until just incorporated.

Add the dry ingredients and beat on low speed until just incorporated.

Add the chocolate chips, beating to combine.

Weigh each cookie dough ball to 130 g (4½ oz). Once all the dough is measured, mould each dough ball into a bird's nest shape and place a frozen salted caramel ball in the centre. Carefully wrap the cookie dough around the salted caramel so it is completely covered. Chill the dough balls in the fridge for at least 3 hours before baking.

When ready to bake, preheat the oven to 180°C (400°F) and line a baking tray with baking paper. Place cookie dough balls onto the tray at least 2 cm (¾") apart and bake for 16–18 minutes until golden on top.

Allow to cool for 10–15 minutes before enjoying. (Try not to be impatient; the cookies need this time to continue cooking at room temperature!)

Once cooled, sprinkle each cookie with sea salt flakes and enjoy!

STORAGE
Once baked, these cookies will last for 5–7 days in an airtight container at room temperature. Alternatively, you can freeze raw dough balls for up to 3 months and bake for a few more minutes from frozen.

Brown Butter Matchadamia Cookies

If your tastebuds are more on the savoury side, then this matcha and macadamia cookie will be right up your alley. If you haven't tried baking with matcha powder before, be sure to get your hands on ceremonial-grade matcha powder for the best results. This is one of those ingredients where quality really matters. The flavour profile of this cookie has nutty, caramelised undertones, thanks to the process of browning the butter. It might take a little longer, but believe me when I say this extra step is so worth it for the final product! The sweet white chocolate chips contrast with the bitterness of the matcha, while the macadamia nuts complete the buttery balancing act.

MAKES: 8–10 COOKIES
PREPARATION TIME: 10 MINUTES
COOKING TIME: 16–18 MINUTES
COOLING TIME: 10–15 MINUTES

200 g (7 oz) unsalted butter
180 g (6¼ oz) light brown sugar
80 g (2¾ oz) caster sugar
1 large egg, room temperature
250 g (9 oz) self-raising flour
200 g (7 oz) plain flour
50 g (1¾ oz) ceremonial-grade matcha powder
pinch of salt
1 teaspoon of baking powder
200 g (7 oz) white chocolate chips
100 g (3½ oz) macadamias, roughly chopped

Start by browning the butter in a small saucepan over medium-high heat. Continually whisk the butter as it melts. Once melted, the butter will begin to foam around the edges. Continue stirring and do not leave the stove unattended. In about 5 minutes, the butter will turn golden brown, resulting in a nutty aroma.

Immediately remove the pan from the heat and pour the butter into a heatproof bowl to cool and stop the cooking process.

Once the butter has cooled, in the bowl of a stand mixer with the paddle attachment, beat the butter and sugars for 3–5 minutes, until light and fluffy.

Add the egg and beat on low speed until just incorporated.

Add the dry ingredients and beat on low speed until just incorporated. Be careful to go slow as the matcha powder will puff up in a green cloud if you're not careful!

Add the chocolate chips and macadamias, beating on low speed to combine.

Weigh each cookie dough ball to 150 g (5¼ oz). Chill in the fridge for at least 3 hours before baking.

When ready to bake, preheat the oven to 180°C (400°F) and line a baking tray with baking paper. Place cookie dough balls onto the tray at least 2 cm (¾") apart and bake for 16–18 minutes until golden on top.

Allow to cool for 10–15 minutes before enjoying. (Try not to be impatient; the cookies need this time to continue cooking at room temperature!)

STORAGE
Once baked, these cookies will last for 5–7 days in an airtight container at room temperature. Alternatively, you can freeze raw dough balls for up to 3 months and bake for a few more minutes from frozen.

Cinnamon Scrolls in Scandinavia

Cinnamon is one of my most loved spices in baking. Not only does it add a flavour dimension no other spice can emulate, but also, the aroma of a fresh batch of cinnamon scrolls baking in your kitchen is enough to brighten anyone's mood.

The Swedes are commonly regarded as the creators of cinnamon scrolls. But if you spend any amount of time exploring Nordic countries, you'll soon come to learn that all of Scandinavia has a strong affinity for these deliciously moreish masterpieces. From Stockholm to Oslo, Helsinki to Copenhagen, you won't find any shortage of cinnamon scrolls, cinnamon rolls or cinnamon buns.

Back in the bakery, we're always looking for new flavour inspiration. A quick scroll (lol) through my old travel journals and I'm never short of ideas. As someone who grew up on an island, the fact that you can cross borders and cultures in just one train ride is totally mind-boggling (even to this day). So I've made no shortage of pilgrimages to Europe under the guise of 'research marketing', tasting my way through countries from north to south, east to west.

As a Virgo who loves a list, I've compiled a list of my favourite bakeries and the creations they are famous for, should you ever wish to follow in my footsteps and eat your weight in sugary, buttery goodness.

EUROPEAN BAKERY BUCKET LIST

1. **Pastéis de Belém, Lisbon** – famous for their pastéis de nata (or Portuguese tart).

2. **Café Sacher Wien, Vienna** – home to the world's best chocolate cake, the original sacher-torte.

3. **La Viña, San Sebastián** – widely renowned as the inventor of the Basque cheesecake.

4. **Fabrique, Stockholm** – famous for sourdough bread baked by time-honoured traditions, but I defy you to leave without one (or two!) of the cardamom, cinnamon or vanilla buns.

5. **Van Stapele Koekmakerij, Amsterdam** – a petite bakery famous for one flavour of cookie, with a line up the street at all hours of the day!

6. **Juno the Bakery, Copenhagen** – famous for their cardamom buns.

7. **Hafiz Mustafa 1864, Istanbul** – a true taste of baklava and Turkish delight.

8. **La Maison Stohrer, Paris** – the oldest patisserie in Paris, famed for its classic French pastries.

9. **La Cannoleria Siciliana, Rome** – serving up the best cannoli in Italy.

10. **Brauð & Co, Reykjavik** – famous about town for its cinnamon scrolls.

11. **Du Pain et des Idées, Paris** – home to what I would regard as the best croissant in Paris.

12. **Pasticceria Marchesi 1824, Milan** – famous for its brioche.

13. **Pierre Hermé, Paris** – iconic French patisserie famous for macarons.

14. **St. John Bakery, London** – the best jam-filled doughnuts in London, plus seasonal specials.

Cinnamon Scroll Cookies

I was scouring my pantry on a Sunday afternoon with a craving for cinnamon scrolls, when I realised I was out of dried yeast. Instead of doing the obvious and driving to the store, I decided to attempt making a cinnamon scroll cookie hybrid. The result of which is this melt-in-mouth white chocolate cookie balanced with a cream cheese centre and a delightful hit of cinnamon paste. Little did I know it would become a crowd favourite when I launched it in the bakery!

MAKES: 8–10 LARGE COOKIES
PREPARATION TIME: 10 MINUTES
COOKING TIME: 16–18 MINUTES
COOLING TIME: 10–15 MINUTES

For the cinnamon paste:
40 g (1½ oz) unsalted butter, room temperature
60 g (2 oz) light brown sugar
4 teaspoons of ground cinnamon

For the cookies:
160 g (5½ oz) cream cheese, chilled
200 g (7 oz) unsalted butter, room temperature
180 g (6¼ oz) light brown sugar
80 g (2¾ oz) caster sugar
1 large egg, room temperature
250 g (9 oz) self-raising flour
200 g (7 oz) plain flour
pinch of salt
1 teaspoon of baking powder
200 g (7 oz) white chocolate chips

First make the cinnamon paste by combining the butter, brown sugar and ground cinnamon in a small bowl. Use a spoon to mix together until fully incorporated and set aside.

Line a baking tray with baking paper and cut small squares of 20 g (¾ oz) cream cheese onto it. Place in the fridge to keep cool while you make the cookie dough.

In the bowl of a stand mixer with the paddle attachment, beat the butter for 2 minutes on medium speed. Add the sugars and beat for a further 3–5 minutes. Scrape down the sides of the bowl to ensure all of the butter is fully incorporated.

Add the egg and beat on low speed until just incorporated.

Add the dry ingredients and beat on low speed until just incorporated.

Add the chocolate chips, beating on low speed to combine.

Weigh each cookie dough ball to 130 g (4½ oz). Once all the dough is measured, mould each dough ball into a bird's nest shape and place the cream cheese in the centre. Spoon around 10 g (½ oz) of cinnamon paste on top before carefully wrapping the cookie dough around the filling so it is completely covered. Chill the dough balls in the fridge for at least 3 hours before baking.

When ready to bake, preheat the oven to 180°C (400°F) and line a baking tray with baking paper. Place cookie dough balls onto the tray at least 2 cm (¾") apart and bake for 16–18 minutes until golden on top.

Allow to cool for 10–15 minutes before enjoying. (Try not to be impatient; the cookies need this time to continue cooking at room temperature!)

STORAGE
Once baked, these cookies will last for 3 days in an airtight container in the fridge.

Gluten-Free New York Cookies (GF)

It took me a long time to land on a perfect gluten-free cookie recipe. In my early days of baking, I would have thought gluten-free baking was super simple: just swap the plain flour for a gluten-free alternative, right? I could not have been more wrong. Due to the drop in protein when using gluten-free flours, recipes need a little extra love to bind the baked goods. For these cookies, the addition of cornflour acts as a thickener, and the increased amount of egg assists in binding the cookie's other ingredients. What you're left with is a delicious gluten-free version of our bestselling New York Cookies.

MAKES: 8–10 LARGE COOKIES
PREPARATION TIME: 10 MINUTES
COOKING TIME: 16–18 MINUTES
COOLING TIME: 10–15 MINUTES

230 g (8 oz) unsalted butter, cold and cubed
130 g (4½ oz) light brown sugar
130 g (4½ oz) caster sugar
2 large eggs, room temperature
440 g (15½ oz) gluten-free plain flour
1 ½ teaspoons of baking powder
27 g (1 oz) cornflour
pinch of salt
300 g (10½ oz) dark chocolate chips
200 g (7 oz) walnuts, roughly chopped

In the bowl of a stand mixer with the paddle attachment, beat the butter for 2 minutes on medium speed. Add the sugars and beat for a further 2–3 minutes. Scrape down the sides of the bowl to ensure all of the butter is fully incorporated.

Add the eggs one at a time on low speed until just incorporated.

Add the dry ingredients and beat until fully incorporated.

On low speed, add the chocolate chips and walnuts to combine.

Weigh each cookie dough ball to 150 g (5 ¼ oz). Chill in the fridge for at least 3 hours before baking.

When ready to bake, preheat the oven to 180°C (400°F) and line a baking tray with baking paper. Place cookie dough balls onto the tray at least 2 cm (¾") apart and bake for 16–18 minutes until golden on top.

Allow to cool for 10–15 minutes before enjoying.
(Try not to be impatient; the cookies need this time to continue cooking at room temperature!)

STORAGE
Once baked, these cookies will last for 5–7 days in an airtight container at room temperature. Alternatively, you can freeze raw dough balls for up to 3 months and bake for a few more minutes from frozen.

My New York Love Affair

New York is often considered the birthplace of food trends and this is never truer than when it comes to baked goods. When I first visited New York City, I was just twenty years old. I arrived during the depths of winter, which to an Australian is more of a joy than a discomfort, as I had never seen snow in a city before.

I fell in love with New York headfirst and in a heartbeat. If love at first sight is to be believed, I found it in Manhattan somewhere between Central Park and Times Square, in a way only a first-timer tourist can. I was enamoured by the city! And that was before I discovered it was home to some of the best bakeries in the world.

After my first visit, I was hooked. I would go on to return a handful of times over the following years, tasking myself with finding the best cookies, ice-cream, croissants and hybrid bakes, such as cruffins and cronuts circa 2013. I took my job particularly seriously, scouring the city as far north as Harlem, all the way down to the Lower East Side. Once I ran out of options in Manhattan I would venture over to Brooklyn, only to start my search once again. All of this in the name of market research in line with my dream to one day open my own bakery.

So, if you find yourself in need of a New York bakery bucket list, your girl has got you covered.

NEW YORK BAKERY BUCKET LIST:

Levain Bakery, various locations

If there's just one bakery you have to visit in the city, let it be a branch of Levain – and yes, let it be for cookies. Although this bakery has expanded its offering to a handful of other bakes, it is their cookies they are known and loved for. The classic choc chip walnut is what sparked my desire to create the world's best cookies back at home in Australia. Levain will forever be my first port of call whenever I return to the city.

Tres Leches Cafe, Harlem

It's no secret that New York City is a cultural melting pot rich in nationalities, religions and languages. Venture north towards Harlem and you will discover the best tres leches cake of your life (a bold claim I'm willing to stand by). As well as the delectably light sponge that's soaked in three different kinds of milk, you will also discover many other authentic Mexican and Dominican sweets.

Magnolia Bakery, various locations

You can't come to New York as a baker and not visit Magnolia Bakery. This is where the world fell in love with cupcakes, popularised by the one and only *Sex and the City* episode where Carrie and Miranda sit outside indulging in what would have to be the best cupcakes in the city (I'm unapologetically biased!). Try the hummingbird cupcake for a taste of Jamaica's speciality pecan pineapple number, or the red velvet for an all-time classic.

Supermoon Bakehouse, Lower East Side

Who knew bakeries could be so trendy? This hidden little gem on the Lower East Side features holographic packaging, a terrazzo countertop and some of the flakiest croissants you'll get your hands on this side of the pond. (Rumour has it the owner trained in Paris.)

Eileen's Special Cheesecake, Nolita

If it's a traditional New York Cheesecake you crave, Eileen's Special Cheesecake has been serving up classic cheesecakes since 1974 and has become a favourite of New Yorkers. Locals and tourists alike will tell you this is where you can get one of the best cheesecakes in the city, and after trying for yourself, you'll soon see why.

BROWNIES & BLONDIES

Every baker needs a great brownie recipe in their repertoire. The popularity of this deliciously decadent treat never ceases to amaze me – we sell truckloads of brownies in the bakery every day. But what is it that makes a perfect brownie? In my opinion, brownies are best fudgey, slightly on the under baked side, and reliant on a night spent in the fridge to set so they melt in your mouth upon impact. Some people prefer their brownies cakey – I do not. But if you sway towards the cakey camp, you can just as easily increase your flour ratio, use baking powder as a leavener, or even just bake your brownie for an extra few minutes. And the secret to achieving a crackly top is to whip your eggs well to incorporate air. Quite often in baking you're told not to over beat the eggs – but brownies are an important exception to the rule. Whisk away!

The Very Best Brownies (GF)

When it comes to naming baking creations, calling anything 'the very best' is an almighty claim. But let me tell you, this brownie is so good that I would nearly go so far as to name it *the only brownie recipe you'll ever need.* With a crackly top and fudgy centre, this brownie is so soft it will quite literally melt away if you let it linger in your mouth long enough (spoiler: you won't). You could open a bakery and just sell these brownies alone, and if I didn't possess the recipe myself, I'd be there lining up ready for you to take my money! And if things couldn't get any better, this recipe is gluten-free, so the GF people in your life can enjoy a square, too.

MAKES: 9 SQUARES IN A 20 CM (8") SQUARE PAN
PREPARATION TIME: 20 MINUTES
COOKING TIME: 25–30 MINUTES
COOLING TIME: 2 HOURS

75 g (2½ oz) dark chocolate chips
170 g (6 oz) unsalted butter, melted
200 g (7 oz) caster sugar
90 g (3 oz) light brown sugar
1 teaspoon of vanilla extract
3 large eggs, room temperature
40 g (1½ oz) cocoa powder
70 g (2½ oz) gluten-free plain flour

Preheat the oven to 160°C (350°F). Grease and line a 20 cm (8") square pan with baking paper, ensuring two sides overhang for easy removal.

Place chocolate chips in a large bowl. Slowly pour melted butter over the top, mixing until the chocolate has melted. Add sugars and vanilla, gently whisking together until fully incorporated.

Add the eggs one at a time, stirring in between. Then sift in the cocoa powder and flour. Stir until just combined.

Pour batter into the prepared pan and bake for 25–30 minutes. (Cooking times will vary depending on your oven; you will know the brownie is ready once it is no longer wobbly in the middle. If you prefer a fudgy texture, bake for 25 minutes; for a more cakey texture, bake for an additional 5 minutes.)

Leave brownie in the pan and transfer to a wire rack to cool completely. This brownie is quite fragile so if you can, transfer to the fridge for at least 2 hours before cutting into squares to serve.

STORAGE
These brownies will keep for up to 5 days if refrigerated in an airtight container. To serve warm, simply reheat in the microwave for 20 seconds before serving. You can also freeze squares of baked brownie for up to 1 month and then thaw at room temperature before enjoying.

CUSTOMISATIONS
These brownies are delicious as they are, but are also perfect for customisations. Frozen raspberries are a delicious addition before baking or, if you prefer some crunch, consider adding 200 g (7 oz) of your favourite nuts to the brownie batter before baking.

Nutella Fudge Brownies (GF)

If the limits of your love for chocolate know no bounds, then stop what you're doing and bake this bad boy, pronto! Nutella has such a creamy, intense hazelnut flavour that you'd think, when matched with chocolate fudge, it would almost be too much.

Surprisingly, it isn't. In fact, it's just the right amount of overdoing it. But if you fancy pushing the boundaries any further, serve this brownie warm with some vanilla ice-cream for a real treat.

MAKES: 9 SQUARES IN A 20 CM (8") SQUARE PAN
PREPARATION TIME: 20 MINUTES
COOKING TIME: 25–30 MINUTES
COOLING TIME: 2 HOURS

75 g (2½ oz) dark chocolate chips
170 g (6 oz) unsalted butter, melted
200 g (7 oz) caster sugar
90 g (3 oz) light brown sugar
1 teaspoon of vanilla extract
3 large eggs, room temperature
40 g (1½ oz) cocoa powder
70 g (2½ oz) gluten-free plain flour
75 g (2½ oz) Nutella spread

vanilla ice-cream, to serve (optional)

Preheat the oven to 160°C (350°F). Grease and line a 20 cm (8") square pan with baking paper, ensuring two sides overhang for easy removal.

Place chocolate chips in a large bowl. Slowly pour melted butter over the top, mixing until the chocolate has melted. Add sugars and vanilla, gently whisking together until fully incorporated.

Add the eggs one at a time, stirring in between. Then sift in the cocoa powder and flour. Stir until just combined.

Pour batter into the prepared pan and swirl the Nutella spread through the batter.

Bake for 25–30 minutes. (Cooking times will vary depending on your oven; you will know the brownie is ready once it is no longer wobbly in the middle. If you prefer a fudgy texture, bake for 25 minutes; for a more cakey texture, bake for an additional 5 minutes.)

Leave brownie in the pan and transfer to a wire rack to cool completely. This brownie is quite fragile so if you can, transfer to the fridge for at least 2 hours before cutting into squares to serve with vanilla ice-cream (optional).

STORAGE
These brownies will keep for up to 5 days if refrigerated in an airtight container. To serve warm, simply reheat in the microwave for 20 seconds before serving. You can also freeze squares of baked brownie for up to 1 month and then thaw at room temperature before enjoying.

CUSTOMISATIONS
If you're feeling creative in the kitchen, this brownie recipe is highly adaptable. You could swap the Nutella spread for peanut butter or Biscoff for an equally delicious bake.

Hazelnut Fudge Brownies

If ever I feel like a loaded brownie, I usually reach for nuts to bring crunch and well-rounded flavour to each bite. Hazelnuts make a great addition to brownies, but if you really want to load them up, try the addition of Ferrero Rochers and hazelnut praline for a death-by-chocolate treat that you won't be able to put down.

MAKES: 9 SQUARES IN A 20 CM (8") SQUARE PAN
PREPARATION TIME: 20 MINUTES
COOKING TIME: 25–30 MINUTES
COOLING TIME: 2 HOURS

75 g (2½ oz) dark chocolate chips
170 g (6 oz) unsalted butter, melted
200 g (7 oz) caster sugar
90 g (3 oz) light brown sugar
1 teaspoon of vanilla extract
3 large eggs, room temperature
70 g (2½ oz) plain flour
40 g (1½ oz) cocoa powder
75 g (2½ oz) hazelnut praline spread
10 Ferrero Rochers, roughly chopped

10 Ferrero Rochers and Nutella, to decorate
 (optional)

Preheat the oven to 160°C (350°F). Grease and line a 20 cm (8") square pan with baking paper, ensuring two sides overhang for easy removal.

Place chocolate chips in a large bowl. Slowly pour the melted butter over the top, carefully mixing until the chocolate has melted. Add the sugars and vanilla extract, gently whisking together until fully incorporated.

Add the eggs one at a time, stirring in between. Then sift in the flour and cocoa powder. Stir until just combined.

Pour the brownie batter into the prepared pan and swirl the hazelnut praline spread through the batter. Place the Ferrero Rochers on top of the brownie and gently push them into the batter.

Bake for 25–30 minutes. (Cooking times will vary depending on your oven; you will know the brownie is ready once it is no longer wobbly in the middle. If you prefer a fudgy texture, bake for 25 minutes; for a more cakey texture, bake for an additional 5 minutes.)

Leave brownie in the pan and transfer to a wire rack to cool completely. This brownie is quite fragile so if you can, transfer to the fridge for at least 2 hours before cutting into squares to serve.

When sliced, stick a Ferrero Rocher onto each brownie with a small blob of Nutella, to decorate (optional).

STORAGE
These brownies will keep for up to 5 days if refrigerated in an airtight container. To serve warm, simply reheat in the microwave for 20 seconds before serving. You can also freeze the baked brownies for up to 1 month and thaw at room temperature before enjoying.

Raspberry Fudge Brownies

I've never been one to overlook the magic that is the pairing of chocolate and raspberry. The tartness of raspberries paired with the decadence of high-quality dark chocolate is a match made in baking heaven. This brownie is no exception. To intensify the raspberry flavour, I've added freeze-dried raspberries to the batter. However, if you cannot source them easily, some extra frozen raspberries will do the trick, as will serving the brownie with freshly whipped cream and fresh raspberries on the side.

MAKES: 9 SQUARES IN A 20 CM (8") SQUARE PAN
PREPARATION TIME: 20 MINUTES
COOKING TIME: 25–30 MINUTES
COOLING TIME: 2 HOURS

75 g (2½ oz) dark chocolate chips
170 g (6 oz) unsalted butter, melted
200 g (7 oz) caster sugar
90 g (3 oz) light brown sugar
1 teaspoon of vanilla extract
3 large eggs, room temperature
40 g (1½ oz) cocoa powder
70 g (2½ oz) plain flour
200 g (7 oz) frozen raspberries
100 g (3½ oz) freeze-dried raspberries (optional)

whipped cream and fresh raspberries, to serve (optional)

Preheat the oven to 160°C (350°F). Grease and line a 20 cm (8" inch) square pan with baking paper, ensuring two sides overhang for easy removal.

Place chocolate chips in a large bowl. Slowly pour the melted butter over the top, carefully mixing until the chocolate has melted. Add sugars and vanilla, gently whisking together until fully incorporated.

Add the eggs one at a time, stirring in between. Then sift in the cocoa powder and flour. Stir until just combined. Add the frozen raspberries and freeze-dried raspberries, if using.

Pour batter into the prepared pan and bake for 25–30 minutes. (Cooking times will vary depending on your oven; you will know the brownie is ready once it is no longer wobbly in the middle.)

Leave brownie in the pan and transfer to a wire rack to cool completely. This brownie is quite fragile so if you can, transfer to the fridge for at least 2 hours before cutting into squares then serve with a dollop of whipped cream and some fresh raspberries on top.

STORAGE
These brownies will keep for up to 5 days if refrigerated in an airtight container. To serve warm, simply reheat in the microwave for 20 seconds before serving. You can also freeze the baked brownies for up to 1 month and thaw at room temperature before enjoying.

Blackout Oreo Brownies

Have you ever wondered why Oreos are black? I did, which is why I ended up creating a range of blackout brownies and cookies for the bakery in celebration of black cocoa, the core ingredient of Oreo biscuits.

Try this black Oreo brownie that has the crunch of Oreos in every bite for a more balanced and less traditionally chocolately brownie.

MAKES: 9 SQUARES IN A 20 CM (8") SQUARE PAN
PREPARATION TIME: 20 MINUTES
COOKING TIME: 25–30 MINUTES
COOLING TIME: 2 HOURS

75 g (2½ oz) dark chocolate chips
170 g (6 oz) unsalted butter, melted
200 g (7 oz) caster sugar
90 g (3 oz) light brown sugar
1 teaspoon of vanilla extract
3 large eggs, room temperature
70 g (2½ oz) plain flour
40 g (1½ oz) black cocoa powder
100 g (3½ oz) Oreos, roughly chopped

Preheat the oven to 160°C (350°F). Grease and line a 20 cm (8") square pan with baking paper, ensuring two sides overhang for easy removal.

Place chocolate chips in a large bowl. Slowly pour the melted butter over the top, carefully mixing until the chocolate has melted. Add the sugars and vanilla, gently whisking together until fully incorporated.

Add the eggs one at a time, stirring in between. Then sift in the flour and black cocoa powder. Stir until just combined.

Pour batter into the prepared pan and push chopped Oreos into it.

Bake for 25–30 minutes. (Cooking times will vary depending on your oven; you will know the brownie is ready once it is no longer wobbly in the middle.)

Leave brownie in the pan and transfer to a wire rack to cool completely. This brownie is quite fragile so if you can, transfer to the fridge for at least 2 hours before cutting into squares to serve.

STORAGE
These brownies will keep for up to 5 days if refrigerated in an airtight container. To serve warm, simply reheat in the microwave for 20 seconds before serving. You can also freeze the baked brownies for up to 1 month and thaw at room temperature before enjoying.

Tiramisu Brownies

When you think about the anatomy of tiramisu and break it down into parts, I think it only makes sense to adapt this Italian classic dessert with a rich, fudgy brownie base – which is precisely why this recipe became an instant hit in the bakery. This brownie is gloriously creamy, decadent and fluffy thanks to the sponge fingers. It requires only a little more effort, but holds the absolute guarantee of impressing your friends.

MAKES: 12 SQUARES IN A 30 × 20 CM (9 × 12")
RECTANGULAR PAN
PREPARATION TIME: 30 MINUTES
COOKING TIME: 25–30 MINUTES
COOLING TIME: OVERNIGHT

For the brownie base:
225 g (8 oz) unsalted butter
140 g (5 oz) 70% dark chocolate
2 teaspoons of espresso powder (or instant coffee)
5 large eggs, room temperature
200 g (7 oz) white sugar
200 g (7 oz) light brown sugar
100 g (3½ oz) plain flour
50 g (1¾ oz) cocoa powder
pinch of salt

For the sponge finger layer:
15–20 sponge fingers
150 ml (5 fl oz) strongly brewed coffee

For the mascarpone layer:
380 ml (13 fl oz) thickened cream
120 g (4¼ oz) icing sugar
2 teaspoons of vanilla extract
340 g (12 oz) mascarpone

cocoa powder, to finish

To make the brownie base:

Preheat the oven to 160°C (350°F). Grease and line a 30 cm × 23 cm (9 × 12") rectangular pan with baking paper, ensuring two sides overhang for easy removal.

In a saucepan, place butter, chocolate and espresso powder and heat on medium-low heat. Stir continuously, until the butter has melted and everything is incorporated. Set aside to cool.

In the bowl of a stand mixer with the paddle attachment, beat the eggs and sugars until light and fluffy (the mixture should almost double in volume).

Pour the cooled chocolate mixture in and continue to mix on a low speed. Add the dry ingredients and whisk until smooth.

Pour batter into the prepared pan and bake for 25–30 minutes. (Cooking times will vary depending on your oven; you will know the brownie is ready once it is no longer wobbly in the middle, but be careful not to overbake.)

Remove from the oven and set aside to cool in the tin while preparing the other layers.

To make the sponge finger layer:

Once the brownie has cooled, it's time to prepare the sponge finger layer. Dip each sponge finger into the strongly brewed coffee – nice and quickly each side so you don't soak them completely.

Place the sponge fingers on top of the brownie (you might have to cut some of them so they fit).

To make the mascarpone layer:

In the bowl of a stand mixer, whisk the thickened cream, icing sugar and vanilla until it starts to thicken slightly.

Add the mascarpone and continue to whisk until the mixture is thick.

STORAGE
These brownies are best enjoyed straight away, but will store for up to 3 days if refrigerated in an airtight container.

CUSTOMISATIONS
If you prefer a boozy tiramisu, add 2 tablespoons of Frangelico or Kahlúa to your freshly brewed coffee and dip your sponge fingers into the mix.

Carefully pour this mixture over the sponge finger layer. Smooth it out with an offset spatula and then allow to set in the fridge for at least a few hours or, even better, overnight.

Once set, carefully lift your brownie out of the pan and dust with cocoa powder. Slice evenly and enjoy!

Red Velvet Cream Cheese Brownies

While some experimental bakers have tried to mess with the combination of red velvet and cream cheese by substituting the cream cheese for something else, I blatantly refuse to do so. In my humble opinion, there is no greater union on planet earth than red velvet and cream cheese. Slightly tart, the red velvet flavour has a hint of cocoa that marries perfectly with the smooth richness of the cream cheese. And what better way to enjoy this combo than in a brownie?

MAKES: 9 SQUARES IN A 20 CM (8") SQUARE PAN
PREPARATION TIME: 30 MINUTES
COOKING TIME: 30–35 MINUTES
COOLING TIME: 3 HOURS

For the brownie layer:
240 g (8½ oz) unsalted butter, melted
365 g (13 oz) caster sugar
3 teaspoons of vanilla extract
6 large eggs, room temperature
1 teaspoon of red food colouring
180 g (6¼ oz) plain flour
1 teaspoon of salt

For the cheesecake layer:
450 g (1 lb) Philadelphia cream cheese, room
 temperature
120 g (4¼ oz) caster sugar
30 g (1 oz) cornflour
3 teaspoons of vanilla extract
150 ml (5 fl oz) thickened cream, room temperature
90 g (3 oz) white chocolate, melted

Preheat the oven to 160° (350°F). Grease and line a 20 cm (8") square pan with baking paper, ensuring two sides overhang for easy removal.

To make the brownie layer:

In the bowl of a stand mixer with a paddle attachment, beat on low-medium the melted butter, sugar and vanilla until combined. Add the eggs one at a time and beat on medium speed for 2–3 minutes. On low speed, add the red food colouring and mix until fully incorporated.

Add the flour and salt, and mix until combined. Pour batter into the prepared pan.

To make the cheesecake layer:

Whisk all ingredients in the bowl of a stand mixer with the whisk attachment. Spoon this mixture over the brownie layer and bake for 30–35 minutes. (Cooking times will vary depending on your oven; you will know the brownie is ready once it is no longer wobbly in the middle.) Cool for at least 3 hours or overnight and cut when completely set.

STORAGE
These brownies are best stored in an airtight container in the fridge for up to 3 days. They can also be frozen for up to 1 month in an airtight container. To thaw, leave the brownies at room temperature for at least 1 hour before enjoying.

The Brookie

Aren't we lucky to live in a world where a brownie and a cookie can coexist in one dessert? The Brookie is the internet's answer to never settling for the status quo and I, for one, am here for the dirty duo. Many moons ago I discovered the infamous 'slutty brownie' online, a brownie-cookie hybrid with a layer of Oreos baked in the centre. The name is a little too ominous for me (at least for a cookbook with my name on it), but The Brookie I bring you here is one and the same – a brownie and a cookie, with a layer of Oreos waiting to be discovered inside.

MAKES: 16 SQUARES IN A 20 CM (8") SQUARE PAN
PREPARATION TIME: 30 MINUTES
COOKING TIME: 30–35 MINUTES
COOLING TIME: 4 HOURS OR OVERNIGHT

For the cookie dough layer:
115 g (4 oz) unsalted butter, room temperature
100 g (3½ oz) dark brown sugar
100 g (3½ oz) granulated sugar
1 large egg, room temperature
1 teaspoon of vanilla extract
140 g (5 oz) plain flour
½ teaspoon of bicarbonate of soda
½ teaspoon of salt
130 g (4½ oz) dark chocolate chips

For the biscuit layer:
16 Oreos

For the brownie layer:
85 g (3 oz) unsalted butter, melted
130 g (4½ oz) dark chocolate, roughly chopped
15 g (½ oz) Dutch cocoa powder
150 g (5¼ oz) granulated sugar
2 large eggs, room temperature
50 g (1¾ oz) plain flour
½ teaspoon of salt

Preheat the oven to 160°C (350°F). Grease and line a 20 cm (8") square pan with baking paper, ensuring two sides overhang for easy removal.

To make the cookie dough:

In the bowl of a stand mixer with the paddle attachment, beat butter and sugars on medium speed until light and fluffy, about 3–4 minutes. On low speed, beat in the egg and vanilla. Add dry ingredients and mix until just combined. Be careful not to over mix. Finally, fold in the chocolate chips.

Transfer the cookie dough to the prepared pan, pressing down evenly. Bake for 8 minutes until just beginning to brown on top. Allow to cool slightly on a wire rack.

To make the brownies:

Pour the melted butter over the chocolate in a large bowl and stir until combined. Add cocoa powder and sugar, whisking until combined. Stir in the eggs, followed by the dry ingredients. Gently fold until combined. Set aside.

Layer Oreos on top of the cookie dough in one layer.

Pour the brownie batter slowly over the Oreos and smooth the top. Bake until a toothpick inserted into the centre of the brownies comes out with moist crumbs, around 20–25 minutes. You'll know the brownie is done when it's no longer wobbly in the centre.

Allow brownies to cool completely on a wire rack, then refrigerate until set for easy cutting, at least 4 hours or overnight. Lift brownies out of the pan carefully and cut with a sharp knife into 16 squares.

STORAGE
Brookies can be kept at room temperature in an airtight container for up to 3 days or up to 5 days if refrigerated.

CUSTOMISATIONS
Just because these stuffed Brookies are usually made with Oreos doesn't mean you can't get creative! Mix it up by trying your favourite biscuits in the centre, such as Tim Tams or, if you prefer, ditching the biscuit layer altogether.

Testing Your Tastebuds in Tokyo

Here's what I love about travel the most: it exposes your senses to new sights, sounds, smells, and my personal favourite – tastes! For me, the excitement of travel comes from discovering new things, and most of my days on the road are usually planned around food. While there is no single place on earth I would say has led to the most discovery, there are certainly a handful of cities, countries and cultures that stand out above the rest. One of these places is Tokyo, the home of anime, karaoke bars, robot restaurants, dizzyingly crowded crosswalks below a sea of electronic advertising and of course, the food. There is no shortage of great places to eat in Tokyo, which is home to an abundance of Michelin-starred restaurants, fine dining sushi-ya, casual izakaya and street food stalls. But the part I love most about the Tokyo food scene, perhaps unsurprisingly, are the sweet offerings.

Satisfying your sweet tooth in Tokyo is an easy task to undertake. No matter the neighbourhood, you're sure to find an endless array of sweets on offer (and in fact, knowing where to start is often the hardest task!). But like any metropolis, restaurants come and go as quickly as the latest food trend, so it is more about knowing what to look for, before deciding where to find it.

Parfait

We'll start with a timeless classic that has been a favourite across the country since its introduction more than 100 years ago. While the origins of parfait began in France, the Japanese parfait goes in a more Americanised direction, only the elements are more delicate and focus heavily on texture to bring this classic dessert to life. Served in a tall glass, a Japanese parfait will encompass a range of seasonal fruits, jellies, ice-cream and some sort of crunch. The whole thing is indulgent in the best kind of way, so don't be afraid to order one to share! If you fancy recreating these masterpieces at home just be sure to include plenty of layers and textures, plus a long dessert spoon to really dive in.

Kakigori

The shaved ice phenomenon in Tokyo borderlines on obsession, with an endless supply of dessert cafes serving up all kinds of creations. While flavours can become as adventurous as the pairing of avocado with pistachio, the most popular are more along the lines of strawberry, mango, green melon and matcha.

Crepes

While it is no secret that crepes originated in France (in Brittany in the thirteenth century), there has been no shortage of crepe stores on this side of the globe for decades. From classic flavours featuring fresh strawberries and cream to more experimental offerings such as tuna and curry sauce, you're guaranteed a sensory discovery inside a Japanese take on the wafer-thin pancakes the world has come to know and love. You will find an endless array of choices located along Takeshita-dori in Harajuku. Just be prepared to wait in line!

Soft Serve

Affectionately known locally as soft cream, at almost every turn in Tokyo there is a soft-serve machine serving up unique flavour combinations, all of which typically start with a milk base. Super creamy Hokkaido milk soft serve should not go overlooked, but it is the matcha soft serve that truly has my heart!

Mochi

As far as traditional Japanese desserts go, it doesn't get more tried-and-true than mochi. This traditional sticky rice dessert is a favourite among locals but has also managed to win the heart of foreigners the world over. There are a variety of ways to enjoy the chewy treat, from traditional jelly-like *warabimochi* to the more dense and chewy *daifuku*, filled with red bean paste.

Matcha White Choc Blondies

Matcha, albeit a flavour I personally cherish and enjoy almost daily, is not everyone's cup of tea (pardon the pun). Matcha as we know it today is a staple in Japanese desserts and widely produced in Japan, which is where I first discovered my love for the earthy flavour. The trick to baking with matcha is to source the highest quality matcha you can, as this is one of those ingredients where quality really matters. In this Matcha White Choc Blondie, I've balanced the earthy bitterness of green tea with the sweetness of white chocolate, complemented by a brown butter base to give the recipe delicious caramel undertones.

MAKES: 9 SQUARES IN A 20 CM (8") SQUARE PAN
PREPARATION TIME: 20 MINUTES
COOKING TIME: 25–30 MINUTES
COOLING TIME: 2 HOURS

120 g (4¼ oz) unsalted butter, cubed
120 g (4¼ oz) white chocolate chips
2 tablespoons of ceremonial-grade
  matcha powder, sifted
200 g (7 oz) granulated sugar
55 g (2 oz) light brown sugar
3 large eggs, room temperature
1 teaspoon of vanilla extract
pinch of salt
120 g (4¼ oz) plain flour

Preheat the oven to 160°C (350°F). Grease and line a 20 cm (8") square pan with baking paper, ensuring two sides overhang for easy removal.

To brown the butter, place in a saucepan and heat over medium heat until it melts. Once melted, the butter will begin to foam around the edges. Stir for about 5 minutes until the butter has turned golden brown. Some foam will subside and you'll see the butter has changed to a toasted brown colour. The butter is browned when it smells nutty. Remove from the stove.

To make matcha chocolate ganache, in a small bowl, sift the matcha powder over the white chocolate and stir. Pour the brown butter over the top and stir until all the chocolate melts. Set aside to cool.

In the bowl of a stand mixer with the beater attachment, combine sugars, eggs, vanilla and salt. Beat until thick and creamy (5–10 minutes).

While mixing, steadily pour in your matcha chocolate ganache. Mix until you have a uniformly green batter.

Lastly, sift the flour into the bowl. Using a spatula, gently fold the flour into the batter and spoon into the prepared pan.

Bake for 25–30 minutes. (Cooking times will vary depending on your oven; you will know the brownie is ready once it is no longer wobbly in the middle.) Allow to cool, then place in the fridge for a few hours to firm up, before slicing and serving.

STORAGE
These brownies will keep for up to 5 days if refrigerated in an airtight container. Alternatively, you can freeze the baked brownies for up to 1 month and thaw at room temperature before enjoying.

Kinder Bueno Blondies

When I first travelled solo to Europe at twenty years of age, I was on the financially strict – but imaginative – student budget, often substituting snacks for meals. I had a particularly hard-to-shake obsession with Kinder chocolates, which came to be my favoured train snack while I hopped from one city to the next. This Kinder Bueno Blondie takes me right back to those train rides, savouring every bite of sweetness while I longingly look out of the window, dreaming of the life in front of me. I think twenty-year-old me would be proud of the bakery owner she became, choosing her happiest place on earth to spend the rest of her days after searching the world for such happiness. Funnily enough, it was right here all along, in the kitchen.

MAKES: 9 SQUARES IN A 20 CM (8") SQUARE PAN
PREPARATION TIME: 30 MINUTES
COOKING TIME: 25–30 MINUTES
COOLING TIME: 2 HOURS

225 g (8 oz) unsalted butter, room temperature
110 g (3¾ oz) caster sugar
110 g (3¾ oz) dark brown sugar
2 teaspoons of vanilla extract
2 large eggs, room temperature
260 g (9 oz) plain flour
1 teaspoon of salt
150 g (5¼ oz) white chocolate chips
200 g (7 oz) Kinder chocolate, broken into pieces
200 g (7 oz) Kinder Bueno, broken into pieces

Preheat the oven to 160°C (350°F). Grease and line a 20 cm (8") square pan with baking paper, ensuring two sides overhang for easy removal.

In the bowl of a stand mixer, beat the softened butter and sugars on medium-high speed until pale and fluffy, about 3–5 minutes. Add vanilla and eggs, one at a time, scraping the bowl well after each addition.

Add flour and salt, and mix all ingredients together on a low speed, until just combined. Fold in white chocolate chips, Kinder chocolate chunks and Bueno pieces. Pour batter into the prepared pan.

Bake for 25–30 minutes, until golden. You'll know the blondie is cooked when it's no longer wobbly in the centre. (If you prefer a fudgy texture, bake for 25 minutes; for a more cakey texture, bake for an additional 5 minutes.)

Allow the blondies to cool in the pan before transferring to the fridge for at least 2 hours, or overnight.

Once cooled completely, remove from the fridge and the baking pan and cut into 9 even pieces.

STORAGE
These blondies will keep for up to 1 week if kept in an airtight container in the fridge. Alternatively, you can freeze the baked blondies for up to 1 month, thawing at room temperature before enjoying.

Raspberry Coconut Blondies

The tropical sweetness of coconut doesn't feature all that often in my baking creations, but that isn't to say I don't love how well it pairs with the tartness of raspberries. This is my modern take on the classic raspberry coconut slice made with jam, which was popular in our household when I was a kid. As I grow older, my own tastes evolve and I'm now more open to fresh berries in my bakes (with a generous supply of white chocolate for good measure, of course).

MAKES: 9 SQUARES IN A 20 CM (8") SQUARE PAN
PREPARATION TIME: 30 MINUTES
COOKING TIME: 25–30 MINUTES
COOLING TIME: 2 HOURS

225 g (8 oz) unsalted butter, room temperature
110 g (3¾ oz) caster sugar
110 g (3¾ oz) dark brown sugar
2 teaspoons of vanilla extract
2 large eggs, room temperature
260 g (9 oz) plain flour
1 teaspoon of salt
150 g (5¼ oz) white chocolate chips
100 g (3½ oz) raspberries, frozen or fresh
50 g (1¾ oz) shredded coconut

Preheat the oven to 160°C (350°F). Grease and line a 20 cm (8") square pan with baking paper, ensuring two sides overhang for easy removal.

In the bowl of a stand mixer with the paddle attachment, beat the butter and sugars on medium-high speed until pale and fluffy, about 3–5 minutes. Add vanilla and eggs, one at a time, scraping the bowl well after each addition.

Add flour and salt, and mix all ingredients together on a low speed, until just combined. Fold in white chocolate chips, raspberries and shredded coconut, being careful not to over mix. Pour the batter into the prepared baking pan.

Bake for 25–30 minutes, until golden.

Allow the blondies to cool in the pan before transferring to the fridge for at least 2 hours, or overnight.

Once cooled completely, remove from the fridge and the baking pan and cut into 9 even pieces.

STORAGE
These blondies will keep for up to 1 week if refrigerated in an airtight container. Alternatively, you can freeze the baked blondies for up to 1 month, thawing at room temperature before enjoying.

Caramilk Blondies

If you haven't heard of Caramilk before, you're not the only one. We are asked every day in the bakery what it is, to which we explain: a caramelised white chocolate – unapologetically sweet and deliciously creamy. This blondie is all of that and more, particularly enjoyable warm from the oven and slightly under baked so it melts away upon impact.

MAKES: 9 SQUARES IN A 20 CM (8") SQUARE PAN
PREPARATION TIME: 30 MINUTES
COOKING TIME: 25–30 MINUTES
COOLING TIME: 2 HOURS

225 g (8 oz) unsalted butter, room temperature
110 g (3¾ oz) caster sugar
110 g (3¾ oz) dark brown sugar
2 teaspoons of vanilla extract
2 large eggs, room temperature
260 g (9 oz) plain flour
1 teaspoon of salt
200 g (7 oz) white chocolate chips
300 g (10½ oz) Caramilk, roughly chopped

Preheat the oven to 160°C (350°F). Grease and line a 20 cm (8") square pan with baking paper, ensuring two sides overhang for easy removal.

In the bowl of a stand mixer with the paddle attachment, beat the butter and sugars on medium-high speed until pale and fluffy, about 3–5 minutes. Add vanilla and eggs, one at a time, scraping the bowl well after each addition.

Add flour and salt, and mix all ingredients together on a low speed, until just combined. Fold in white chocolate chips and roughly chopped Caramilk pieces. Pour the batter into the prepared baking pan.

Bake for 25–30 minutes, until golden.

Allow the blondies to cool in the pan, before transferring to the fridge for at least 2 hours, or overnight.

Once cooled completely, remove from the fridge and the baking pan and cut into 9 even pieces.

STORAGE
These blondies will keep for up to 1 week if refrigerated in an airtight container. Alternatively, you can freeze the baked blondies for up to 1 month, thawing at room temperature before enjoying.

Biscoff Blondies

I only discovered Biscoff when I was travelling around Belgium in search of the best waffles and frites the country had to offer. It was at a breakfast buffet in Antwerp where my love affair began. Since then, I've managed to incorporate Biscoff spread and biscuits into just about any baked good you could imagine. This blondie is a particularly loaded affair, with a hefty dose of both spread and biscuits – a tribute to all my fellow Biscoff lovers out there.

MAKES: 9 SQUARES IN A 20 CM (8") SQUARE PAN
PREPARATION TIME: 30 MINUTES
COOKING TIME: 25–30 MINUTES
COOLING TIME: 2 HOURS

225 g (8 oz) unsalted butter, room temperature
110 g (3¾ oz) caster sugar
110 g (3¾ oz) light brown sugar
2 teaspoons of vanilla extract
2 large eggs, room temperature
260 g (9 oz) plain flour
1 teaspoon of salt
150 g (5¼ oz) white chocolate chips
200 g (7 oz) Biscoff biscuits, crushed
200 g (7 oz) Biscoff spread

Preheat the oven to 160°C (350°F). Grease and line a 20 cm (8") square pan with baking paper, ensuring two sides overhang for easy removal.

In the bowl of a stand mixer with the paddle attachment, cream the butter and sugars on medium-high speed until pale and fluffy, about 3–5 minutes. Add vanilla and eggs, one at a time, scraping the bowl well after each addition.

Add flour and salt, and mix all ingredients together on a low speed, until just combined. Fold in white chocolate chips and crushed Biscoff biscuits. Transfer the batter into the prepared pan.

Pour Biscoff spread on top of the blondie and use a spoon to gently swirl through the blondie.

Bake for 25–30 minutes, until golden. (Cooking times will vary depending on your oven; you will know the brownie is ready once it is no longer wobbly in the middle. If you prefer a fudgy texture, bake for 25 minutes; for a more cakey texture, bake for an additional 5 minutes.)

Allow the blondies to cool in the pan, before transferring to the fridge for at least 2 hours, or overnight.

Once cooled completely, remove from the fridge and the baking pan and cut into 9 even pieces.

STORAGE
These blondies will keep for up to 1 week if refrigerated in an airtight container. Alternatively, you can freeze the baked blondies for up to 1 month, thawing at room temperature before enjoying.

Cake Batter Blondies

Like in many families, birthdays were a big deal in our household when I was growing up. It was the one day of the year when you could choose what was for dinner and you could absolutely guarantee there would be cake. As I grow older, I try to keep that same birthday magic alive for my friends and family by baking a treat on their special day. These Cake Batter Blondies make the perfect birthday gift (and best of all, you can enjoy the leftovers!).

MAKES: 9 SQUARES IN A 20 CM (8") SQUARE PAN
PREPARATION TIME: 30 MINUTES
COOKING TIME: 25–30 MINUTES
COOLING TIME: 2 HOURS

225 g (8 oz) unsalted butter, room temperature
110 g (3¾ oz) caster sugar
110 g (3¾ oz) dark brown sugar
2 teaspoons of vanilla extract
2 large eggs, room temperature
260 g (9 oz) plain flour
1 teaspoon of salt
200 g (7 oz) white chocolate chips
100 g (3½ oz) rainbow Jimmies

Preheat the oven to 160°C (350°F). Grease and line a 20 cm (8") square pan with baking paper, ensuring two sides overhang for easy removal.

In the bowl of a stand mixer with the paddle attachment, beat the butter and sugars on medium-high speed until pale and fluffy, about 3–5 minutes. Add vanilla and eggs, one at a time, scraping the bowl well after each addition.

Add flour and salt, and mix all ingredients together on a low speed, until just combined. Fold in white chocolate chips and rainbow Jimmies. Pour the batter into the prepared baking pan.

Bake for 25–30 minutes, until golden.

Allow the blondies to cool in the tin, before transferring to the fridge for at least 2 hours, or overnight.

Once cooled completely, remove from the fridge and the baking pan and cut into 9 even pieces.

STORAGE
These blondies will keep for up to 1 week if refrigerated in an airtight container. Alternatively, you can freeze the baked blondies for up to 1 month, thawing at room temperature before enjoying.

BROOKI'S TIP
I use Jimmies when baking because rainbow nonpareils (small balls) will bleed through the blondie when you fold them in. Longer sprinkles (sometimes called 'Jimmies'), on the other hand, will hold their shape in the cake batter.

CUPCAKES

Small in size but big in flavour, cupcakes are a great way to celebrate the special moments in life without the hassle of creating a full-sized cake. These petite portions are always a popular choice among partygoers, too, as you can enjoy a variety instead of settling for just one flavoured cake. So be sure to bake a few different recipes for your next gathering, as a little variety goes a long way for that sweet end to your shindig. The secret of a great cake sponge, in my opinion, is in the wet ingredients. The inclusion of oil will yield a much more moist texture, which stays fresher and tender for far longer than a butter cake. Butter cakes have a place in my kitchen too, however, offering a superior fat flavour and evenly melting texture with every bite. Let's dive in to the most joyous chapter of all!

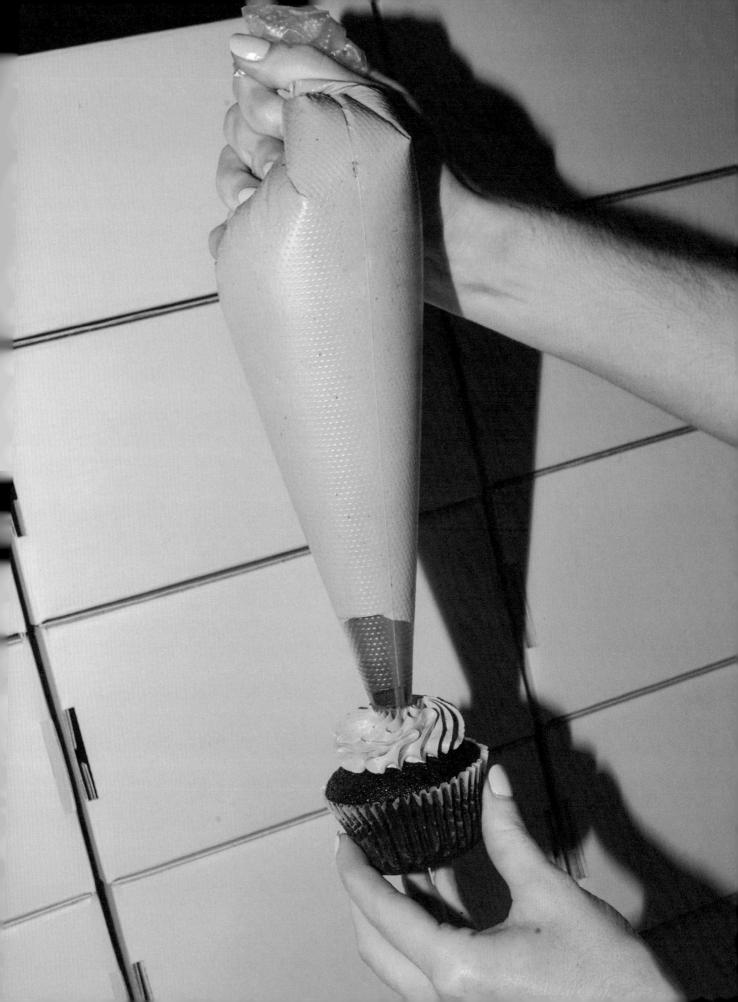

Vanilla Cupcakes

There's nothing overly fancy about these Vanilla Cupcakes, except for the fact that they stay fresh for up to 1 week without losing moisture if kept in an airtight container. This alone makes them a great choice for bakers who like to have everything done in advance, as you can make these cupcakes a few days before an event without anyone ever knowing!

MAKES: 12 CUPCAKES
PREPARATION TIME: 15 MINUTES
COOKING TIME: 16 MINUTES
COOLING TIME: 1 HOUR

For the cupcakes:
160 g (5½ oz) flour
200 g (7 oz) caster sugar
1¼ teaspoons of baking powder
pinch of salt
125 ml (4 fl oz) milk
55 ml (2 fl oz) vegetable oil
1 large egg, room temperature
120 ml (4 fl oz) water

For the buttercream:
250 g (9 oz) unsalted butter, room temperature
150 g (5¼ oz) icing sugar, sifted
1 teaspoon of vanilla extract

rainbow sprinkles, to decorate

To make the cupcakes:

Preheat the oven to 170°C (375°F). Line a 12-cup cupcake pan with cupcake liners.

Sift the flour, sugar, baking powder and salt together in a bowl and set aside.

In the bowl of a stand mixer with the paddle attachment, beat the wet ingredients on low speed, until just combined.

Add the dry ingredients and mix on low speed, until just combined.

Using a large ice-cream scoop, evenly portion the batter between the cupcake liners. Ideally, I like to fill them to just over halfway (to be precise, halfway between half-full and three-quarters full). This cupcake batter is particularly runny, so you might prefer to pour the batter into the pan from a jug instead. Gently tap the cupcake pan on the bench to evenly distribute the batter.

Bake the cupcakes for 16 minutes. Remove from the oven and allow to cool completely before icing with the buttercream.

To make the buttercream:

In the bowl of a stand mixer with the paddle attachment, beat the butter on medium speed until pale and fluffy, about 5 minutes. On low speed, add the icing sugar and mix until combined.

Increase the speed of the mixer to high and mix for a further 5 minutes. Lower the speed to add the vanilla and mix for 1 more minute.

Transfer the buttercream into a piping bag fitted with a large round piping tip. Swirl the icing on top and sprinkle with rainbow sprinkles to finish.

STORAGE
These cupcakes have an unusually long shelf life thanks to the oil and water, making them perfect for baking ahead or large-batch baking. Store iced cupcakes in an airtight container for up to 7 days at room temperature. Alternatively, you can freeze cooked, uniced cupcakes the day they're baked for up to 1 month. To thaw, bring them to room temperature for 1 hour before icing with buttercream.

BROOKI'S TIP
For evenly baked cupcakes, it is important to mix this batter properly before each new ingredient is added to the mix. Be careful not to over mix and always be sure to tap your cupcake pan on the bench before baking.

Chocolate Cupcakes

I've been using this same recipe without tweaks for almost a decade – it really is just that good. I like to use it as the base for all of our chocolate cupcake varieties in the bakery, switching up the fillings and buttercream for new flavour creations.

MAKES: 12 CUPCAKES
PREPARATION TIME: 15 MINUTES
COOKING TIME: 16–18 MINUTES
COOLING TIME: 1 HOUR

For the cupcakes:
170 g (6 oz) plain flour
pinch of salt
1 teaspoon of bicarbonate of soda
85 g (3 oz) unsalted butter, room temperature
225 g (8 oz) light brown sugar
2 large eggs, room temperature
1 teaspoon of vanilla extract
50 g (1¾ oz) Dutch cocoa powder
110 g (3¾ oz) sour cream
1 tablespoon of instant coffee dissolved in
  130 ml (4¼ fl oz) hot water

1 batch of Chocolate Buttercream (see page 280)

50 g (1¾ oz) grated chocolate, to decorate

Preheat the oven to 180°C (400°F). Line a 12-cup cupcake pan with cupcake liners.

Whisk the flour, salt and bicarbonate of soda together in a bowl and set aside.

In the bowl of a stand mixer with the paddle attachment, beat the butter and sugar together on high speed until light and fluffy, about 5 minutes. Scrape down the sides of the bowl as required.

On low speed, beat in the eggs one at a time until just combined, and then add the vanilla.

On low speed, add the cocoa powder and mix until combined. Then add the sour cream one-third at a time, alternating with the dry ingredients. This ensures you do not over mix the batter, mixing until just combined. The batter will be thick at this stage.

On the lowest speed, add the hot coffee, aiming to pour between the side of the bowl and the paddle attachment, and scraping down the sides of the bowl as you go.

Using a large ice-cream scoop, evenly portion the batter between the cupcake liners. Ideally, I like to fill them to just over halfway (to be precise, halfway between half-full and three-quarters full). Lightly tap the cupcake pan on the bench before baking, to evenly distribute the batter.

Bake the cupcakes for 16–18 minutes or until a skewer comes out clean. Remove from the oven and allow to cool completely before icing with the Chocolate Buttercream.

To decorate, transfer the buttercream into a piping bag fitted with your desired piping tip, pipe onto the top of each cupcake and then simply sprinkle with grated chocolate.

STORAGE
These cupcakes can be stored uniced for up to 3 days in an airtight container at room temperature. Alternatively, you can freeze cooked, uniced cupcakes the day they're baked for up to 1 month. To thaw, bring them to room temperature for 1 hour before icing with buttercream.

Red Velvet Cupcakes

I'm always excited on days when there is a leftover Red Velvet Cupcake or two in the bakery, as these are one of my favourites. (Due to their popularity, this rarely happens!) These cupcakes are soft and moist, perfectly matched with a silky cream cheese frosting. They've become a classic on our cupcake menu and I dare say that won't change anytime soon.

MAKES: 12 CUPCAKES
PREPARATION TIME: 15 MINUTES
COOKING TIME: 18–20 MINUTES
COOLING TIME: 1 HOUR

For the cupcakes:
160 g (5½ oz) plain flour
2 tablespoons of cornflour
1½ teaspoons of unsweetened cocoa powder, sifted
1 teaspoon of bicarbonate of soda
½ teaspoon of salt
45 g (1½ oz) unsalted butter, room temperature
180 g (6¼ oz) caster sugar
120 ml (4 fl oz) vegetable oil
2 large eggs, room temperature
1½ teaspoons of vanilla extract
¾ teaspoon of white vinegar
1 teaspoon of red food colouring gel
110 ml (3¾ fl oz) buttermilk, room temperature

For the cream cheese frosting:
225 g (8 oz) Philadelphia cream cheese, room temperature
100 g (3½ oz) unsalted butter, room temperature
1 teaspoon of vanilla extract
300 g (10½ oz) icing sugar, sifted

4 tablespoons of red velvet crumbs or
 12 maraschino cherries, to decorate

To make the cupcakes:

Preheat the oven to 170°C (375°F). Line a 12-cup cupcake pan with cupcake liners.

Sift the flour, cornflour, cocoa powder, bicarbonate of soda and salt together in a bowl and whisk to combine, then set aside.

In the bowl of a stand mixer with the paddle attachment, beat the butter and sugar together on high speed until light and fluffy, about 5 minutes. Scrape down the sides of the bowl then slowly pour in the oil, beating to combine.

Beat in the eggs, vanilla, vinegar and food colouring on low speed, until just combined.

On low speed, add the dry ingredients and slowly pour in the buttermilk, until just combined.

Using a large ice-cream scoop, evenly portion the batter between the cupcake liners. Ideally, I like to fill them to just over halfway (to be precise, halfway between half-full and three-quarters full). Gently tap the cupcake pan on the bench before baking, to evenly distribute the batter.

Bake the cupcakes for 18–20 minutes. Remove from the oven and allow to cool completely before icing with the cream cheese frosting.

To make the cream cheese frosting:

In the bowl of a stand mixer with the paddle attachment, beat the cream cheese and butter on medium speed until smooth, about 3 minutes.

Add the vanilla and beat well. Gradually add the sugar on low speed until fully incorporated, before increasing to high speed. Continue to beat on high speed until smooth and creamy, about 5 minutes.

Transfer the frosting into a piping bag fitted with a round piping tip. Pipe frosting onto the cupcakes and sprinkle with red velvet crumbs or place a maraschino cherry on top.

STORAGE
Iced cupcakes will keep for up to 3 days in the fridge in an airtight container. Cooked, uniced cupcakes can be frozen the day they're baked for up to 3 months in an airtight container. To thaw, bring them to room temperature for 1 hour before icing with cream cheese frosting.

BROOKI'S TIP
It is important to sift the cocoa powder and whisk the dry ingredients together in this cupcake recipe, as you don't want the cocoa to clump in the cupcake batter.

BAKED WITH
LOVE
IN BRISBANE

Hummingbird Cupcakes

If there is just one recipe in my collection I beg you not to overlook, it is this one. Unless you grew up in the Caribbean or within walking distance of a Magnolia Bakery in New York City, you might not have heard of hummingbird cake before. Originating from Jamaica, hummingbird is now a staple flavour of southern states in the USA and a seasonal special at my bakery. It is also the one item in the bakery I cannot bake without eating at least three cupcakes in quick succession. Yes, it really is *that good!* The secret to a great hummingbird is in the texture, with a lighter crumb than, say, carrot cake (see page 122), but enough silkiness to melt in your mouth thanks to the vegetable oil in place of butter for the fat component. Whichever way you look at it, this cake is seriously addictive. You have been warned!

MAKES: 12 CUPCAKES
PREPARATION TIME: 20 MINUTES
COOKING TIME: 18–20 MINUTES
COOLING TIME: 1 HOUR

For the cupcakes:
180 g (6¼ oz) plain flour
½ teaspoon of ground cinnamon
½ teaspoon of bicarbonate of soda
½ teaspoon of salt
150 ml (5 fl oz) vegetable oil
240 g (8½ oz) caster sugar
2 large eggs, room temperature
1 teaspoon of vanilla extract
200 g (7 oz) very ripe banana, mashed
  (about 2 large bananas)
110 g (3¾ oz) crushed pineapple in juice,
  drained and roughly chopped (about half a can)
60 g (2 oz) pecans, roughly chopped

For the cream cheese frosting:
225 g (8 oz) Philadelphia cream cheese, room
  temperature
100 g (3½ oz) unsalted butter, room temperature
1 teaspoon of vanilla extract
300 g (10½ oz) icing sugar, sifted

12 pecan halves, to decorate

To make the cupcakes:

Preheat the oven to 170°C (375°F). Line a 12-cup cupcake pan with cupcake liners.

In a large bowl, whisk together the flour, cinnamon, bicarbonate of soda and salt. Set aside.

In the bowl of a stand mixer with the paddle attachment, beat the oil and sugar until smooth on medium speed, about 3 minutes. Lower the speed and add the eggs. Beat on medium speed until light and fluffy, about 2 minutes.

Add the vanilla extract, banana and pineapple, and one-third of the dry ingredients. Continue adding the dry ingredients one-third at a time, until fully incorporated. Mix in the pecans.

Using a large ice-cream scoop, evenly portion the batter between the cupcake liners. Ideally, I like to fill them to just over halfway (to be precise, halfway between half-full and three-quarters full). Gently tap the cupcake pan on the bench before baking, to evenly distribute the batter.

Bake for 18–20 minutes, or until a skewer comes out clean.

Remove from the oven and allow to cool completely before icing with cream cheese frosting.

STORAGE
Store iced cupcakes in an airtight container for up to 3 days in the fridge.

To make the cream cheese frosting:

In the bowl of a stand mixer with the paddle attachment, beat the cream cheese and butter on medium speed until smooth, about 3 minutes.

Add the vanilla and beat well. Gradually add the sugar on low speed until fully incorporated, before increasing to high speed. Continue to beat on high speed until smooth and creamy, about 5 minutes.

Transfer the frosting into a piping bag fitted with a round piping tip. Pipe frosting onto the cupcakes and top each one with a pecan kernel to finish.

Berry Cheesecake Cupcakes

In spring and summer, this is one of our bestselling items in the bakery full stop. The marriage of a berry cupcake with a cream cheese frosting really just tips our customers over the edge, to the point where I've had multiple customers return to grab a box of six after initially purchasing a single cupcake. The biscuit crumble on top gives this cupcake the perfect buttery crunch.

MAKES: 12 CUPCAKES
PREPARATION TIME: 15 MINUTES
COOKING TIME: 16 MINUTES
COOLING TIME: 1 HOUR

For the cupcakes:
160 g (5½ oz) plain flour
200 g (7 oz) caster sugar
1 teaspoon of baking powder
pinch of salt
125 ml (4 fl oz) milk
55 ml (2 fl oz) vegetable oil
1 large egg, room temperature
120 ml (4 fl oz) water
100 g (3½ oz) mixed berries, fresh or frozen

For the biscuit crumb:
50 g (1¾ oz) digestive biscuits, crushed
55 g (1¾ oz) unsalted butter, melted

For the cream cheese frosting:
225 g (8 oz) Philadelphia cream cheese,
 room temperature
100 g (3½ oz) unsalted butter, room temperature
1 teaspoon of vanilla extract
300 g (10½ oz) icing sugar, sifted

fresh berries, to finish

To make the cupcakes:

Preheat the oven to 170°C (375°F). Line a 12-cup cupcake pan with cupcake liners.

Sift the flour, sugar, baking powder and salt together in a bowl and set aside.

In the bowl of a stand mixer with the paddle attachment, beat the wet ingredients on low speed, until just combined.

Add the dry ingredients and mix on low speed, until just combined. Fold in the berries.

Using a large ice-cream scoop, evenly portion the batter between the cupcake liners. Ideally, I like to fill them to just over halfway (to be precise, halfway between half-full and three-quarters full). This cupcake batter is particularly runny, so you might prefer to pour the batter from a jug instead. Gently tap the cupcake pan on the bench to evenly distribute the batter.

Bake the cupcakes for 16 minutes. Remove from the oven and allow to cool completely before icing.

To make the biscuit crumb:

Mix the crushed biscuits and melted butter together until they reach a crumb texture (I like to use my hands for this one!).

To make the cream cheese frosting:

In the bowl of a stand mixer with the paddle attachment, beat the cream cheese and butter on medium speed until smooth, about 3 minutes.

Add the vanilla and beat well. Gradually add the sugar on low speed until fully incorporated, before increasing to high speed. Continue to beat on high speed until smooth and creamy, about 5 minutes.

Transfer the frosting into a piping bag fitted with a round piping tip. Pipe the frosting onto the cupcakes and top with fresh berries and biscuit crumb.

STORAGE
Store iced cupcakes in an airtight container in the fridge for up to 3 days.

Black Forest Cupcakes

There's something very European about a Black Forest gateau, and not just because it originates from Germany. This cherry-packed chocolate cream cake is often found in old-school bakeries that specialise in European bakes, which is why it has the power to take me straight back to my days wandering around the German countryside in search of the local bäckerei. This is the ideal cupcake at Christmas, when a total of no-one is watching their waistline.

MAKES: 12 CUPCAKES
PREPARATION TIME: 30 MINUTES
COOKING TIME: 16–18 MINUTES
COOLING TIME: 1 HOUR

For the chocolate cupcakes:
170 g (6 oz) plain flour
1 teaspoon of bicarbonate of soda
pinch of salt
85 g (3 oz) unsalted butter, room temperature
225 g (8 oz) light brown sugar
2 large eggs, room temperature
1 teaspoon of vanilla extract
50 g (1¾ oz) Dutch cocoa powder
110 g (3¾ oz) sour cream
1 tablespoon of instant coffee
  dissolved in 130 ml (4½ fl oz) hot water

For the cherry filling:
200 g (7 oz) pitted cherries
25 g (¾ oz) caster sugar
1 tablespoon of cornflour
1 teaspoon of vanilla extract
1 tablespoon of cherry liqueur (optional – I use kirsch)

For the cream frosting:
300 ml (10 fl oz) double cream
1 tablespoon of icing sugar
1 teaspoon of vanilla extract

12 maraschino cherries, to decorate
25 g (¾ oz) dark chocolate shavings, to decorate

STORAGE
Store iced cupcakes in an airtight container in the fridge for up to 2 days.

BROOKI'S TIP
The cupcakes and cherry filling can be made in advance, but the cream frosting is best made fresh on the day.

To make the chocolate cupcakes:

Preheat the oven to 170°C (375°F). Line a 12-cup cupcake pan with cupcake liners.

Whisk the flour, bicarbonate of soda and salt together in a bowl and set aside.

In the bowl of a stand mixer with the paddle attachment, beat the butter and sugar together on high speed until light and fluffy, about 5 minutes. Scrape down the sides of the bowl as required.

On low speed, beat in the eggs one at a time, followed by the vanilla, mixing until just combined.

On low speed, add the cocoa powder and mix until combined. Then add the sour cream one-third at a time, alternating with the dry ingredients. This ensures you do not over mix the batter, mixing until just combined. The batter will be thick at this stage.

On the lowest speed, slowly add the hot coffee, aiming to pour between the side of the bowl and the paddle attachment, scraping down the sides of the bowl as required.

Using a large ice-cream scoop, evenly portion the batter between the cupcake liners. Ideally, I like to fill the pans to just over halfway (to be precise, halfway between half-full and three-quarters full). Gently tap the cupcake pan on the bench before baking, to evenly distribute the batter.

Bake the cupcakes for 16–18 minutes or until a skewer comes out clean. Remove from the oven and allow to cool completely.

Meanwhile, make the cherry filling and cream frosting.

To make the cherry filling:

Place all ingredients in a saucepan over medium heat and stir until bubbling. Allow to simmer for 5–10 minutes, until the sauce thickens.

Set aside to cool completely.

To make the cream frosting:

Place the double cream, icing sugar and vanilla in the bowl of a stand mixer with the whisk attachment. Whip until thick.

To assemble:

Using a round piping tip, core the centre of each cupcake and pipe a small amount of cherry filling into the cavity.

Place the cream frosting into a piping bag and pipe swirls onto each cupcake.

Decorate cupcakes with a maraschino cherry and a sprinkle of dark chocolate shavings.

Banoffee Pie Cupcakes

For me, there is no greater invention than the banoffee pie. I adore toffee-flavoured anything, but to combine that with a biscuit base, whipped cream and banana is truly something to behold. Enter: the Banoffee Pie Cupcake.

MAKES: 12 CUPCAKES
PREPARATION TIME: 30 MINUTES
COOKING TIME: 16–18 MINUTES
COOLING TIME: 1 HOUR

For the cupcakes:
190 g (6¾ oz) plain flour
1 teaspoon of baking powder
1 teaspoon of bicarbonate of soda
½ teaspoon of salt
350 g (12¼ oz) very ripe banana, mashed
  (about 3 large bananas)
85 g (3 oz) unsalted butter, melted
135 g (4¾ oz) light brown sugar
1 large egg, room temperature
1 teaspoon of vanilla extract
2 tablespoons of full cream milk

For the biscuit crumb:
50 g (1¾ oz) digestive biscuits, crushed
55 g (1¾ oz) unsalted butter, melted

For the caramel filling:
½ batch of Salted Caramel Sauce (see page 300),
  without the salt added

For the caramel buttercream:
½ batch of Cream Cheese Frosting (see page 287)
½ batch of Salted Caramel Sauce (see page 300),
  without the salt added

To make the cupcakes:

Preheat the oven to 170°C (375°F). Line a 12-cup cupcake pan with cupcake liners.

Whisk the flour, baking powder, bicarbonate of soda and salt together in a bowl and set aside.

In the bowl of a stand mixer with the paddle attachment, beat the banana, butter and sugar together on high speed until light and fluffy, about 5 minutes. Scrape down the sides of the bowl as required.

Beat in the egg and vanilla on low speed, mixing until just combined.

On low speed, add the dry ingredients and slowly pour in the milk, mixing until combined.

Using a large ice-cream scoop, evenly portion the batter between the cupcake liners. Ideally, I like to fill them to just over halfway (to be precise, halfway between half-full and three-quarters full). Gently tap the cupcake pan on the bench before baking, to evenly distribute the batter.

Bake the cupcakes for 16–18 minutes. Remove from the oven and allow to cool completely.

Meanwhile, make the biscuit crumb, caramel filling and caramel buttercream.

To make the biscuit crumb:

Mix the crushed biscuits and melted butter together until they reach a crumb texture (I like to use my hands for this one!).

To make the caramel filling:

Prepare a batch of Salted Caramel Sauce but do not add the salt. Allow to cool completely before using.

STORAGE
Store these cupcakes for up to 5 days in an airtight container at room temperature, out of direct sunlight.

To assemble:

Using a round piping tip, core the centre of each cupcake to leave a hole in the middle.

Transfer half a batch of Salted Caramel Sauce into a piping bag fitted with a round piping tip and pipe a generous amount of caramel into the cavity of each cupcake.

To make the caramel buttercream:

In the bowl of a stand mixer with the paddle attachment, beat half a batch of Cream Cheese Frosting with half a batch of Salted Caramel Sauce for 2 minutes.

Transfer the buttercream into a piping bag fitted with your preferred piping tip. Swirl on top of each cupcake and sprinkle over biscuit crumb, to finish.

Cookie Dough Cupcakes

Edible cookie dough has had quite a revival in pop culture, which is why we made an adaptation of our favourite Vanilla Cupcakes to include this new craze. When consuming raw dough, just be sure to omit the eggs and heat-treat the flour so it is safe for consumption. All the instructions you'll need are below.

MAKES: 12 CUPCAKES
PREPARATION TIME: 1 HOUR
COOKING TIME: 16 MINUTES
COOLING TIME: 1 HOUR

For the edible cookie dough:
115 g (4 oz) unsalted butter, room temperature
110 g (3¾ oz) light brown sugar
50 g (1¾ oz) caster sugar
1 teaspoon of vanilla extract
1 tablespoon of full cream milk
120 g (4¼ oz) heat-treated plain flour
 (see Brooki's Tip below)
85 g (3 oz) chocolate chips

For the cupcakes:
180 g (6¼ oz) plain flour
1½ teaspoons of baking powder
pinch of salt
115 g (4 oz) unsalted butter, room temperature
200 g (7 oz) caster sugar
2 large eggs + 1 egg white, room temperature
120 ml (4 fl oz) full cream milk, room temperature
1 tablespoon of vanilla extract

For the buttercream:
250 g (9 oz) unsalted butter, room temperature
150 g (5¼ oz) icing sugar, sifted
1 teaspoon of vanilla extract
1 teaspoon of cookie batter flavouring (optional)

STORAGE
Store iced cupcakes in an airtight container for up to 3 days at room temperature.

BROOKI'S TIP
To heat-treat flour so it is safe to consume without baking, preheat the oven to 180°C (400°F). Line a tray with baking paper and spread out the flour in an even layer. Bake for 10 minutes and allow to cool before using.

To make the edible cookie dough:

In the bowl of a stand mixer fitted with the paddle attachment, cream the butter and sugars on high speed until light and fluffy, about 2 minutes. Add the vanilla and milk, and mix until just combined.

Add the heat-treated flour and salt. Mix on high until the mixture is fluffy, before folding in the chocolate chips. Refrigerate for 10–20 minutes to firm up before using your hands to roll into 12 bite-size balls.

To make the cupcakes:

Preheat the oven to 170°C (375°F). Line a 12-cup cupcake pan with cupcake liners.

Sift the flour, baking powder and salt together in a bowl and set aside.

In the bowl of a stand mixer with the paddle attachment, beat the remaining cupcake ingredients on low speed, until just combined.

Add the dry ingredients and mix on low speed, until just combined.

Using a large ice-cream scoop, evenly portion the batter between the cupcake liners. Ideally, I like to fill them to just over halfway (to be precise, halfway between half-full and three-quarters full). This cupcake batter is particularly runny, so you might prefer to pour the batter into the pan from a jug instead. Gently tap the cupcake pan on the bench before baking, to evenly distribute the batter.

Bake the cupcakes for 16 minutes. Remove from the oven and allow to cool completely before icing with the buttercream.

To make the buttercream:

In the bowl of a stand mixer with the paddle attachment, beat the butter on medium speed until pale and fluffy, about 5 minutes. On low speed, add the icing sugar and mix until combined.

Increase the speed of the mixer to high and mix for a further 5 minutes. Lower the speed to add the vanilla and flavouring (if using), and mix for 1 minute.

Transfer the buttercream into a piping bag fitted with your preferred piping tip. Swirl the buttercream onto the cupcakes and place a cookie dough ball on top.

MINI MASTERCLASS:

PERFECTLY PORTIONED CUPCAKES

When it comes to cupcakes, there are a few handy hints I have learned over the years of working in a bakery that I'd love you to know. If you fancy yourself a cupcake connoisseur and want to create perfectly portioned cupcakes with a soft, bouncy sponge, here are my fail-safe (and no longer) secrets:

Be careful not to over beat the cake batter. If you've ever wondered why cake recipes mention 'not to over beat' a batter, there's a good reason! Once the eggs are incorporated, it is important not to continue beating the batter and trapping unnecessary air into the cake sponge (or, in this instance, cupcake sponge). Too much air in your batter will cause the cake to rise too quickly in the baking process and, in turn, it will deflate from the quick rise. Instead you want to mix your cake batter until just combined, so there is no unnecessary air inside that will lead to a collapse.

Use an ice-cream scoop with a release function to portion the batter evenly. I always aim for my cupcake pans to be just a smidge under three-quarters full (to be precise, halfway between half-full and three-quarters full). Any more and they'll pour over the edges during the bake; any less and they won't meet the fringe of the cupcake liner.

Before putting the cupcakes in the oven, gently tap the pan a few times on the bench to release any air and evenly distribute the batter. This will allow your cupcakes to rise evenly and come out perfectly every time.

CAKES

Whether you're celebrating a birthday, wedding or any other major moment in life, nothing commemorates a celebration quite like a cake. With layers of freshly made sponge nestled in between rich and creamy buttercream, a cake is a signifying moment to be shared with friends and family, sparking memories for years to come.

Fluffy Vanilla Cake

While I loved chocolate cake as a child, I grew into my love affair with vanilla cake through adulthood. Light, buttery and with melt-in-mouth consistency, this Fluffy Vanilla Cake is hard to beat. Matched with a silky buttercream, it is ripe for recipe adaptation: you can mix in fresh or frozen berries, or switch up the buttercream flavours as you fancy.

SERVES: 12–14
PREPARATION TIME: 30 MINUTES
COOKING TIME: 24–26 MINUTES

For the cake:
430 g (15 oz) plain flour
1 teaspoon of salt
2 teaspoons of baking powder
¾ teaspoon of bicarbonate of soda
345 g (12 oz) unsalted butter,
  room temperature and cubed
400 g (14 oz) caster sugar
4 large eggs, room temperature
1 tablespoon of vanilla extract
360 ml (12 fl oz) buttermilk, room temperature

For the buttercream:
450 g (1 lb) unsalted butter, room temperature
600 g (1 lb 5 oz) icing sugar
2 teaspoons of vanilla essence

STORAGE
This cake will keep for up to 5 days in an airtight container in the fridge.

BROOKI'S TIP
If you don't have buttermilk handy, it's really easy to make some yourself at home. Just pour 10 ml (2 teaspoons) of lemon juice or white vinegar into 350 ml (11½ fl oz) of room-temperature milk and stir. Allow to sit for 5 minutes before using (you will notice the milk will curdle and thicken, giving the same effect as buttermilk in this recipe).

To make the vanilla cake:

Preheat the oven to 170°C (375°F). Grease and line two 20 cm (8") round cake tins.

Whisk the flour, salt, baking powder and bicarbonate of soda into a bowl and set aside.

In the bowl of a stand mixer with the paddle attachment, beat the butter and sugar together on high speed until light and fluffy, about 5 minutes. Scrape down the sides of the bowl as required.

Beat in the eggs and vanilla on low speed, mixing until just combined. Do not worry if the mixture curdles, it is normal!

On low speed, add the dry ingredients and then slowly pour in the buttermilk, mixing until combined.

Pour the batter evenly into the cake tins. Bake for 24–26 minutes or until a cake skewer comes out clean.

Remove from the oven and place on a wire rack. Allow to cool completely in the tins before icing. (If you're in a hurry, you can speed up this process by placing your cakes in the freezer to chill quicker.)

To make the buttercream:

In the bowl of a stand mixer with the paddle attachment, beat the butter on medium speed until pale and fluffy. On low speed, add the icing sugar and mix until combined.

Increase the speed of the mixer to high and beat for a further 5 minutes. Lower the speed to add the vanilla and mix for 1 more minute.

To assemble:

Once the cakes are completely cooled, remove from the tins. Using a bread knife, slice off the tops of the cakes to create a flat surface, and then cut each cake into two layers. Place one layer on your cake turntable and dollop a generous portion of buttercream in the centre. Use an offset spatula to evenly distribute the buttercream over the top.

Stack each layer one at a time, placing buttercream in between each one and smoothing out before adding the next cake. Spread the remaining buttercream on top and around the sides.

Refrigerate the cake for at least 1 hour before slicing, as this cake needs some time to chill before serving so it holds its shape when cut.

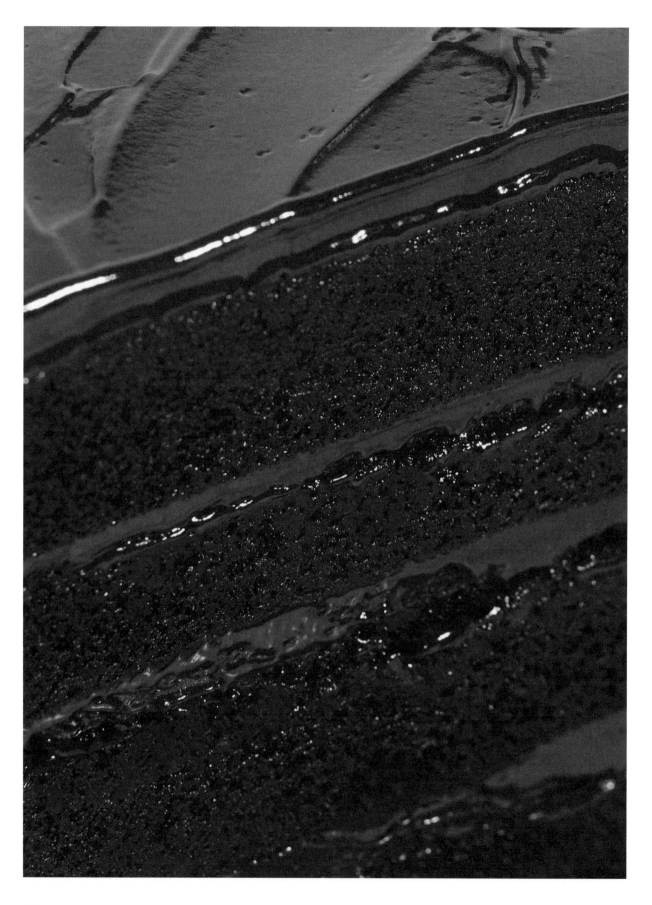

The Best Ever Chocolate Cake

When I eat a chocolate cake, I want it to tick every box. The perfect chocolate cake recipe in my eyes has a moist crumb, intensely rich chocolate taste, and must be easy to make. This chocolate cake has each of these qualities in abundance, and will leave every one of your party guests asking for seconds! Trust me, I've never left a party with leftovers, nor will you.

SERVES: 12–14
PREPARATION TIME: 30 MINUTES
COOKING TIME: 50–55 MINUTES

For the chocolate ganache:
540 ml (18¼ fl oz) thickened cream
1 teaspoon of vanilla bean paste or vanilla extract
60 g (2 oz) liquid glucose
1.1 kg (2 lb 6 oz) milk chocolate, broken into pieces

For the chocolate cake:
420 g (15 oz) plain flour
110 g (3¾ oz) Dutch cocoa powder
15 g (½ oz) bicarbonate of soda
1 teaspoon of baking powder
420 g (15 oz) caster sugar
2 teaspoons of salt
120 ml (4 fl oz) vegetable oil
2 large eggs, room temperature
120 ml (4 fl oz) buttermilk
1 teaspoon of vanilla essence
120 ml (4 fl oz) hot water

To make the chocolate ganache:

As the ganache requires 3 hours to set, I recommend making it first. Place the cream, vanilla and glucose in a saucepan and heat over medium heat. Bring to the boil.

Place the chocolate in a heatproof bowl and pour the hot cream mixture over the top, leaving to sit for 2 minutes before stirring to combine.

Cover the chocolate ganache with plastic wrap, making sure the plastic touches the top to prevent a skin from forming. Leave the ganache at room temperature for approximately 3 hours, or until firm enough to spread. In the meantime, make the cakes.

To make the chocolate cake:

Preheat the oven to 150°C (300°F).

Grease two 15 cm (6") round cake tins with vegetable oil spray, then line the bases with baking paper.

Place the flour, cocoa powder, bicarbonate of soda and baking powder into a bowl. Add the sugar and salt, then set aside.

In the bowl of a stand mixer with the whisk attachment, beat the vegetable oil, eggs, buttermilk and vanilla for 1 minute on medium speed.

Lower the speed, then add the dry ingredients and mix until just combined. With the mixer on the lowest setting, carefully pour in the hot water and mix until combined.

Divide the batter evenly between the two cake tins, then bake for 50–55 minutes, or until a skewer comes out clean.

Allow the cakes to cool at room temperature until the tins are cool to touch, then place them in the freezer for a minimum of 1 hour to cool completely.

→

To assemble:

Once the cakes are completely cooled, remove from the tins and use a bread knife to slice off the tops of the cakes to create a flat surface. Cut each cake evenly into three layers, giving you six layers of cake in total.

Place one layer on your cake turntable and dollop a generous portion of chocolate ganache in the centre. Use an offset spatula to evenly distribute the ganache.

Stack another cake layer on top and cover with ganache. Repeat with the remaining layers, placing ganache in between each one and smoothing out before adding the next layer. Spread the remaining ganache around the sides of the cake.

Transfer to a serving plate, slice and enjoy!

STORAGE
This cake is best enjoyed the same day you make it, but you can easily store the leftovers. This cake will keep for up to 3 days at room temperature in an airtight container (out of direct sunlight). Alternatively, store it in the fridge for up to 7 days in an airtight container.

BROOKI'S TIP
If you don't plan on eating this cake on the same day or next day, then I'd like to introduce you to your new best friend in baking: cake soak. Cake soak (also known as simple syrup) is a great way to extend the life of a cake when baking ahead of time, as it will ensure the cake sponge remains fresher for longer. It's super simple to make – place 50 g (1¾ oz) of sugar and 50 ml (2 tablespoons) of water in a microwave-safe bowl and heat in 30-second bursts until the sugar dissolves.

Birthday Cake

If you've got a friend or family member to celebrate, nothing says birthday more than rainbow sprinkles. This cake has birthday written all over it, so I really couldn't think of a more suitable name for this celebration cake that has layers and layers of rainbow sprinkles, topped with more rainbow sprinkles for good measure.

SERVES: 12–14
PREPARATION TIME: 30 MINUTES
COOKING TIME: 24–26 MINUTES

For the cake:
430 g (15 oz) plain flour
1 teaspoon of salt
2 teaspoons of baking powder
¾ teaspoon of bicarbonate of soda
345 g (12 oz) unsalted butter, room temperature
400 g (14 oz) caster sugar
4 large eggs, room temperature
1 tablespoon of vanilla extract
360 ml (12 fl oz) buttermilk, room temperature
150 g (5¼ oz) rainbow Jimmies

For the buttercream:
450 g (1 lb) unsalted butter, room temperature
600 g (1 lb 5 oz) icing sugar
1 teaspoon of vanilla essence

rainbow Jimmies and 7 maraschino cherries (optional), to decorate

STORAGE
This cake will keep for up to 5 days in an airtight container in the fridge.

BROOKI'S TIP
I use Jimmies when baking because rainbow nonpareils (small balls) will bleed through the cake when you fold them in. Longer sprinkles (sometimes called 'Jimmies'), on the other hand, will hold their shape in the cake batter.

To make the cake:

Preheat the oven to 170°C (375°F). Grease and line three 20 cm (8") round cake tins.

Whisk the flour, salt, baking powder and bicarbonate of soda together in a bowl and set aside.

In the bowl of a stand mixer with the paddle attachment, beat the butter and sugar together on high speed until light and fluffy, about 5 minutes. Scrape down the sides of the bowl as required.

Beat in the eggs and vanilla on low speed, mixing until just combined.

On low speed, add the dry ingredients then slowly pour in the buttermilk, mixing until combined. Fold in the rainbow Jimmies.

Pour the batter evenly into the cake tins. Bake for 24–26 minutes or until a cake skewer comes out clean.

Remove from the oven and place on a wire rack. Allow to cool completely in the tins before icing. (If you're in a hurry, you can speed up this process by placing your cakes in the freezer to chill quicker.)

To make the buttercream:

In the bowl of a stand mixer with the paddle attachment, beat the butter on medium speed until pale and fluffy, about 5 minutes. On low speed, add the icing sugar and mix until combined.

Increase the speed of the mixer to high and beat for a further 5 minutes. Lower the speed to add the vanilla and mix for 1 more minute.

To assemble:

Once the cakes are completely cooled, remove from the tins. Using a bread knife, slice off the tops of the cakes to create a flat surface. Place one cake on your cake turntable and dollop a generous portion of buttercream in the centre. Use an offset spatula to evenly distribute the buttercream over the top.

Stack each cake one at a time, placing buttercream in between each layer and smoothing out before adding the next cake. Spread the remaining buttercream on top and around the sides of the cake.

Before the icing has set, decorate with more rainbow Jimmies on the sides of the cake. Using your preferred piping tip and leftover buttercream, pipe swirls onto the top of the cake and top with maraschino cherries plus some more rainbow Jimmies, if desired.

Refrigerate the cake for at least 1 hour before slicing, as this cake needs some time to chill before serving so it holds its shape when cut.

Carrot Cake

Whenever I walk into a bakery for a pick-me-up, carrot cake is my endgame. It doesn't matter what else that bakery is famous for, I'm going to walk out with carrot cake every single time. This Carrot Cake is one of my favourite recipes of all time, but I must be transparent with the carrot cake enthusiasts out there: it does not contain sultanas. Feel free to mix some in – 75 g (2½ oz) would do the trick – but, as a personal preference, I like my carrot cake without (blasphemy, I know!).

SERVES: 8–10
PREPARATION TIME: 20 MINUTES
COOKING TIME: 35–40 MINUTES

For the cake:
240 g (8½ oz) plain flour
1 teaspoon of baking powder
1 teaspoon of ground cinnamon
½ teaspoon of salt
250 ml (8 fl oz) canola oil
350 g (12¼ oz) caster sugar
3 large eggs, room temperature
1½ teaspoons of vanilla extract
220 g (7¾ oz) grated carrot
440 g (15½ oz) crushed pineapple in juice, drained and roughly chopped (1 can)
125 g (4½ oz) toasted pecans, roughly chopped
75 g (2½ oz) shredded coconut

1 batch of Cream Cheese Frosting (see page 287)

50 g (1¾ oz) toasted pecans, roughly chopped, to decorate (see Brooki's tip below)

To make the carrot cake:

Preheat the oven 160°C (350°F). Grease and line two 22 cm (8") round cake tins.

Whisk the flour, baking powder, cinnamon and salt together in a small bowl and set aside.

In the bowl of a stand mixer with the paddle attachment, beat together the oil and sugar for a few minutes on medium speed.

Add the eggs one at a time, beating until incorporated. Add the vanilla and beat for 2 minutes.

Gradually add the dry ingredients, beating on medium speed until incorporated. Fold in the carrot, pineapple and juice, pecans and coconut.

Pour batter evenly into the cake tins and bake for 35–40 minutes, or until a skewer comes out clean.

Remove from the oven and allow the cakes to cool in their tins for 1 hour, before transferring to a wire rack to cool completely before icing.

To assemble:

Once the cakes are completely cooled, use a bread knife to slice off the tops of the cakes to create a flat surface. (For a four-layer cake, cut each cake in half.)

Place one layer on your cake turntable and dollop a generous portion of cream cheese frosting in the centre. Use an offset spatula to evenly distribute the frosting over the top.

Stack each layer one at a time, placing frosting in between each layer and smoothing out before adding the next layer. Use the remaining frosting on top and sprinkle with toasted pecans.

STORAGE
Store for up to 3 days in an airtight container in the fridge.

BROOKI'S TIP
To toast pecans at home, preheat the oven to 180°C (350°F). Line a baking tray with baking paper and spread pecans over in a single layer. Bake for 15 minutes, or until lightly browned.

Triple Berry Cream Cake

Strawberries and cream was one of my favourite flavour combinations growing up, especially when it came to cake. There's just no reason not to love the sweetness of strawberries amplified by velvety whipped cream, and matched with a melt-in-mouth butter cake. But as I have grown older, I've learned to love the tartness of other berries, too – such as raspberries, blueberries and blackberries. This Triple Berry Cream Cake is just as the name suggests: a mixed berry take on the classic strawberry shortcake.

SERVES: 12–14
PREPARATION TIME: 30 MINUTES
COOKING TIME: 24–26 MINUTES

1 batch of Berry Compote (see page 294)

For the cake:
430 g (15½ oz) plain flour
1 teaspoon of salt
2 teaspoons of baking powder
¾ teaspoon of bicarbonate of soda
345 g (12 oz) unsalted butter, room temperature
400 g (14 oz) caster sugar
3 large eggs + 2 egg whites, room temperature
1 tablespoon of vanilla extract
360 ml (12 fl oz) buttermilk, room temperature
300 g (10½ oz) mixed berries, fresh or frozen

For the buttercream:
450 g (1 lb) unsalted butter, room temperature
800 g (1 lb 12 oz) icing sugar
2 teaspoons of vanilla essence
3 tablespoons of thickened cream

150 g (5¼ oz) fresh mixed berries, to decorate (optional)

To make the cake:

Preheat the oven to 170°C (375°F). Grease and line two 22 cm (8") round cake tins.

Whisk the flour, salt, baking powder and bicarbonate of soda together in a bowl and set aside.

In the bowl of a stand mixer with the paddle attachment, beat the butter and sugar together on high speed until light and fluffy, about 5 minutes. Scrape down the sides of the bowl as required.

On low speed, beat in the eggs one at a time, followed by the egg whites and vanilla, mixing until just combined.

On low speed, add the dry ingredients and slowly pour in the buttermilk, mixing until combined. Gently fold in the berries.

Pour the batter evenly into the cake tins. Bake for 24–26 minutes or until a cake skewer comes out clean.

Remove from the oven and place cake tins on a wire rack. Allow to cool completely in the tins before icing. (If you're in a hurry, you can speed up this process by placing your cakes in the freezer to chill quicker.)

To make the buttercream:

In the bowl of a stand mixer with the paddle attachment, beat the butter on medium speed until pale and fluffy, about 5 minutes. On low speed, add the icing sugar and mix until combined.

Increase the speed of the mixer to high and beat for a further 5 minutes. Lower the speed to add the vanilla and cream, before increasing the speed to mix for another few minutes, until the buttercream is lighter in colour and texture.

STORAGE
This cake will keep for up to 3 days in an airtight container in the fridge.

To assemble:

Once the cakes are completely cooled, remove from the tins. Using a bread knife, slice off the tops of the cakes to create a flat surface and then carefully cut the cakes in half to create four cake layers.

Place one layer on your cake turntable and dollop a generous portion of buttercream on top, and use an offset spatula to evenly distribute it in a ring shape so you create a well in the centre. Fill the well with some Berry Compote, being careful not to overfill the cake with the compote, or the filling will spill out the sides.

Stack each layer with the buttercream and compote.

Apply a small amount of buttercream on top and around the sides of the cake to crumb coat the cake (see page 137). Freeze for 15 minutes before decorating the cake with the remaining buttercream.

Top with fresh mixed berries, if desired, to finish.

Chocolate Raspberry Layer Cake

This cake barely needs an introduction, as it is all in the name. There's something so beautiful about the harmony between rich dark chocolate and a tart fruit like raspberries, which has to be one of my favourite flavour combinations of all time. If you love a rich chocolate cake but want to surprise your guests with something extra special, then this cake is for you.

SERVES: 12–14
PREPARATION TIME: 1 HOUR
COOKING TIME: 24–26 MINUTES

For the chocolate ganache:
550 g (1 lb 3 oz) dark chocolate, roughly chopped
270 ml (9½ fl oz) thickened cream
½ teaspoon of vanilla extract
30 g (1 oz) liquid glucose

For the raspberry filling:
50g (1¼ oz) caster sugar
1 tablespoon of cornflour
2 teaspoons of water
225 g (8 oz) raspberries, fresh or frozen

For the cake:
420 g (15 oz) plain flour
420 g (15 oz) caster sugar
110 g (3¾ oz) Dutch cocoa powder
3 teaspoons of bicarbonate of soda
1 teaspoon of baking powder
2 teaspoons of salt
120 ml (4 fl oz) vegetable oil
2 large eggs, room temperature
120 ml (4 fl oz) buttermilk
1 teaspoon of vanilla essence
120 ml (4 fl oz) hot water

For the chocolate buttercream:
340 g (12 oz) unsalted butter, room temperature
340 g (12 oz) dark chocolate, melted
35 g (1¼ oz) Dutch cocoa powder
690 g (1 lb 8 oz) icing sugar
150 ml (5 fl oz) thickened cream

fresh raspberries, to decorate

To make the chocolate ganache:

Place the chocolate in a heatproof bowl and set aside.

Place the cream in a heatproof bowl and microwave for 15-second intervals until it just begins to bubble (about 45 seconds). Alternatively, you can heat the cream over medium-high heat in a saucepan until it starts to boil.

Pour the hot cream over the chocolate chips and leave for a few minutes before mixing to combine. Stir in the vanilla essence and liquid glucose. Cover the chocolate ganache with plastic wrap, making sure the plastic touches the top to prevent a skin from forming. Leave the ganache at room temperature for approximately 3 hours, or until firm enough to spread. In the meantime, make the filling and cakes.

To make the raspberry filling:

Place the sugar, cornflour and water into a saucepan and heat over medium. Stir continuously until the sugar begins to melt.

Add the raspberries and stir to coat in the mixture. Continue cooking until the raspberries soften (about 5 minutes).

Remove from the heat, strain to remove the seeds and allow to cool in the fridge.

To make the chocolate cake:

Preheat the oven to 180°C (400°F). Grease and line two 22 cm (8") round cake tins and set aside.

Whisk the flour, sugar, cocoa, bicarbonate of soda, baking powder and salt in a large bowl. Set aside.

In the bowl of a stand mixer with the paddle attachment, beat together the vegetable oil, eggs, buttermilk and vanilla essence. Add the dry ingredients and mix to combine.

With the mixer on the lowest setting, slowly pour the hot water into the batter. Mix until everything is well combined.

Pour the batter evenly into the prepared cake tins.

Bake for 22–25 minutes or until a skewer comes out clean. Remove from the oven and allow to cool for a few minutes, transferring to a wire rack to cool completely in the tins.

To make the chocolate buttercream:

In the bowl of a stand mixer with the paddle attachment, beat the butter on high speed for 5 minutes.

On low speed, gently pour in the melted chocolate and continue to mix until combined. Add the cocoa powder and mix well.

Add the icing sugar in small batches, followed by the thickened cream. Mix until everything is incorporated and the buttercream is light and fluffy.

Transfer to a piping bag. (I like to use a 2A tip for this cake.)

To assemble:

Using a bread knife, slice off the tops of the cakes to create a flat surface, then cut each cake in half to create four layers. Place the first layer on a cake board.

Pipe the buttercream around the outer rim of the first layer, to make a dam for the ganache and raspberry filling.

Spread the chocolate ganache inside the ring of buttercream, and place a few spoonfuls of raspberry filling over it in the centre.

Place the next layer on top and repeat the process until all four cakes are stacked.

Use the remaining chocolate buttercream to crumb coat the cake (see page 137). Place in the fridge to set, about 1 hour.

Use the remaining chocolate ganache to drizzle a chocolate drip on the cake and garnish with raspberries.

STORAGE
This cake will keep for up to 3 days in an airtight container in the fridge.

Lemon Raspberry Cake

During the warmer months in Australia, I have a tendency to add raspberries to anything (everything!). There's a lot to be grateful for by way of fresh produce and baking is a great way to maximise the magic of summer by highlighting the flavours that are in season. This lemon raspberry cake does just that by combining fresh raspberries with the zingy zest of lemon, which is often the upgrade from a traditional vanilla cake a summer garden party needs.

SERVES: 12–14
PREPARATION TIME: 30 MINUTES
COOKING TIME: 24–26 MINUTES

For the lemon cake:
350 g (12¼ oz) plain flour
2½ teaspoons of baking powder
½ teaspoon of bicarbonate of soda
½ teaspoon of salt
225 g unsalted butter, room temperature
350 g (12¼ oz) caster sugar
3 large eggs, room temperature
2 teaspoons of vanilla extract
240 ml (8 fl oz) buttermilk
80 ml (3 fl oz) fresh lemon juice
250 g (9 oz) raspberries, fresh or frozen
zest of 2 lemons

For the cream cheese buttercream:
180 g (6¼ oz) unsalted butter, room temperature
300 g (10½ oz) Philadelphia cream cheese, room temperature
600 g (1 lb 5 oz) icing sugar, sifted

fresh raspberries, to decorate (optional)

To make the lemon cake:

Preheat the oven to 170°C (375°F). Grease and line three 20 cm (8") round cake tins.

Whisk the flour, baking powder, bicarbonate of soda and salt together in a bowl and set aside.

In the bowl of a stand mixer with the paddle attachment, beat the butter and sugar together on high speed until light and fluffy, about 5 minutes. Scrape down the sides of the bowl as required.

Beat in the eggs and vanilla on low speed, mixing until just combined. Do not worry if the mixture curdles, this is normal!

On low speed, add the dry ingredients then slowly pour in the buttermilk and lemon juice, mixing until combined. Fold in the raspberries and lemon zest.

Pour the batter evenly into the cake tins. Bake for 24–26 minutes or until a cake skewer comes out clean.

Remove from the oven and place on a wire rack. Allow to cool completely in the tins before icing. (If you're in a hurry, you can speed up this process by placing your cakes in the freezer to chill quicker.)

To make the cream cheese buttercream:

In the bowl of a stand mixer fitted with the paddle attachment, beat the butter on medium speed until pale and fluffy. Add the cream cheese and beat until fully combined.

On low speed, add the icing sugar and mix until combined.

Increase the speed of the mixer to high and mix for a further 5 minutes. Lower the speed to add the lemon juice and mix for 1 more minute.

To assemble:

Once the cakes are completely cooled, remove from the tins. Using a bread knife, slice off the tops of the cakes to create a flat surface. Place one cake on your cake turntable and dollop a generous portion of buttercream in the centre. Use an offset spatula to evenly distribute the buttercream over the top.

Stack each cake one at a time, placing buttercream in between each layer and smoothing out before adding the next cake. Spread buttercream on top and around the sides of the cake, and then pipe swirls of buttercream on top and decorate with fresh raspberries, if using.

Refrigerate the cake for at least 1 hour before slicing, as this cake needs some time to chill before serving so it holds its shape when cut.

STORAGE
This cake will keep for up to 5 days in an airtight container in the fridge.

Persian Love Cake

I can't believe it has taken me until this section of the book to mention this, but I am a seriously devoted dinner party host. Give me a theme and I'll conquer it; give me a cuisine and I'll recipe test for weeks in advance. That is precisely how I discovered Persian Love Cake (*kayk-e eshgh*), a moist almond cake soaked in lemon and rosewater syrup. While the origins are contested, this cake is the perfect way to end a Persian dinner party, as it is the ideal companion to a menu rich in fragrant spices and aromas.

SERVES: 8–12
PREPARATION TIME: 20 MINUTES
COOKING TIME: 50 MINUTES

For the cake:
195 g (6¾ oz) plain flour
265 g (9¼ oz) almond meal
2 teaspoons of baking powder
½ teaspoon of bicarbonate of soda
1 teaspoon of salt
115 g (4 oz) unsalted butter, room temperature
300 g (10½ oz) caster sugar
zest of 1 orange
½ teaspoon of cardamom
½ teaspoon of nutmeg
4 large eggs, room temperature
240 g (8½ oz) plain yogurt
2 teaspoons of rosewater

For the syrup:
80 ml (3 fl oz) lemon juice
70 g (2½ oz) caster sugar
1 teaspoon of rosewater

For the icing:
110 g (3¾ oz) icing sugar, sifted
1½ teaspoons of rosewater
1 tablespoon of lemon juice

handful edible dried rose petals and 75 g (2½ oz) roughly chopped pistachios, to finish

To make the cake:

Preheat the oven to 180°C (400°F). Grease and line a 22 cm (8") round cake tin with baking paper on the base.

Whisk the flour, almond meal, baking powder, bicarbonate of soda and salt in a bowl. Set aside.

In the bowl of a stand mixer with the paddle attachment, beat the butter on medium-high speed until fluffy, about 2 minutes. Add the sugar, orange zest, cardamom and nutmeg, and beat on high speed for another 2 minutes.

Add the eggs on low speed and mix until just combined. Scrape down the sides of the bowl to ensure everything is incorporated.

Add the yogurt and rosewater, mixing until just combined. Scrape the bowl again to ensure all ingredients are fully mixed.

Add the dry ingredients on low speed, being careful not to over mix.

Pour the batter evenly into the prepared cake tin. Bake for around 50 minutes, or until a skewer comes out clean.

Remove from the oven and allow to cool for 10–20 minutes before placing the cake on a wire rack to cool completely out of the tin.

To make the syrup:

Heat the lemon juice and sugar in a small saucepan over a medium heat, stirring until the sugar has dissolved.

Remove from the heat and add the rosewater.

Allow to cool before pouring over the cake.

STORAGE
This cake is best served immediately. Leftovers can be stored at room temperature for 2 days. Alternatively, you can freeze on the same day you bake it, defrosting before pouring over the syrup and decorating.

To make the icing:

Whisk together the icing sugar, rosewater and lemon juice until completely smooth.

To assemble:

Once the cake has cooled, pour the icing on top and sprinkle with rose petals and pistachios before it sets.

CAKE CUTTING, STACKING AND CRUMB COATING

The secret to making perfect cakes is simple: take it one step at a time. Too often, I see cake makers rush the process of stacking and crumb coating a cake, which makes it a whole lot harder to decorate in the final stages. The good news is, I've got lots of tips and tricks in the cake department from years of making cakes for customers – often up to fifty cakes a day!

STEP ONE: BAKE YOUR CAKES

I'm going to tell you a little secret that may or may not change your life. Almost no-one in the professional baking space bakes their cakes on the same day they stack, crumb coat and decorate them. (That is, of course, unless you are in a frantic rush to replace a missing cake order!)

Baking cakes a day, week or even a month in advance is totally acceptable, as the cakes in this book freeze well with no compromise on taste. To freeze cakes for icing later, allow them to cool completely before wrapping in plastic wrap (ensure every part of the cake is tightly covered) and sitting them in the freezer on a flat surface. To thaw out, remove the cakes from the freezer at least 1–2 hours before you wish to decorate them, so they are not too firm when you cut them.

STEP TWO: CUT YOUR CAKES

When you are ready to ice your cakes, place each cake on a rotating cake turntable and gently cut off the domed top with a bread knife to create a perfectly flat surface. This is also the stage when you cut individual cakes into layers. If you'd like to avoid the domes altogether, try baking your cakes at a slightly lower temperature and for longer. This may take a little trial and error, depending on your oven (just ensure a skewer comes out clean to check when the cake is baked).

STEP THREE: SOAK YOUR CAKES

A little sugar soak goes a long way in cake decorating, especially if you are working a day in advance. It's a big ol' secret of commercial bakeries to extend the shelf life on cakes and better yet, it's super simple to make! Simply combine sugar and water in a ratio of 1:1. For example, place 50 g (1¾ oz) of sugar and 50 ml (2 tablespoons) of water in a microwave-safe bowl and heat in 30-second bursts until the sugar dissolves (or heat gently on the stove). Allow to cool and then use a spoon to drizzle over each cake layer, allowing the syrup to soak into the cake, before you ice it.

STEP FOUR: STACK YOUR CAKES

It is easier to stack and crumb coat a slightly chilled cake – whether it has been placed in the fridge for a few hours before stacking (airtight to prevent it from drying out), or whether it has been recently removed from the freezer and is still a bit on the colder side. Handling chilled cakes means the cakes will crumble less, so if you work quickly, it will be easier to stack layers of cake on top of one another, with buttercream and fillings in between.

STEP FIVE: CRUMB COAT

Crumb coating is a thin layer of buttercream that acts as a wall to trap in all the cake crumbs. It's an essential step of cake making for perfectly smooth edges, so be sure not to skip it! Simply spoon some buttercream onto the top of the cake and use an offset spatula to spread evenly around the cake. Once the cake is completely covered, use a flat cake scraper to remove any excess buttercream. Continue until all of the sides and top of the cake are smooth before placing in the fridge to set.

STEP SIX: DECORATE YOUR CAKE

Now comes the fun part! Once your crumb coated cake has set in the fridge (I allow a couple of hours minimum), it's time to decorate. Portion your buttercream into separate bowls for each colour you plan to create. Add a few drops of colour to each bowl and mix well before you start decorating. Use an offset spatula to completely coat the cake and use a flat cake scraper to remove any excess. Place your preferred tip in the base of a piping bag to pipe your favourite patterns and designs.

CAKE IS THE ANSWER, NO MATTER THE QUESTION.

CHEESECAKES

Nothing beats biting into a slice of freshly made cheesecake. With so many variations, from baked to chilled, all the way through to specialty creations such as light and fluffy Basque cheesecake and New York's densely decadent take on this classic, there's a whole world of pillowy melt-in-mouth indulgence ready to be discovered in this chapter. Some techniques take a little longer to execute, but I promise they're worth the effort. The simplest cheesecake recipes here can be thrown together late in the evening and chilled overnight, ready to be enjoyed for the following day's celebrations.

Mixed Berry Cheesecake

When summer hits in Australia, I hit the kitchen to make this classic no-bake cheesecake. This is the easiest cheesecake you will ever make, plus it's a guaranteed crowd-pleaser.

SERVES: 8–10
PREPARATION TIME: 15 MINUTES
CHILLING TIME: OVERNIGHT

250 g (9 oz) digestive biscuits
125 g (4½ oz) unsalted butter, melted
4 tablespoons of cold water
3 teaspoons of gelatine powder
500 g (1 lb 1oz) Philadelphia cream cheese, room
  temperature
140 g (5 oz) caster sugar
500 ml (17 fl oz) thickened cream
200 g (7 oz) Raspberry Coulis (see page 293)

250 g (9 oz) fresh berries, to decorate
icing sugar, to decorate (optional)

Grease and line the base of a 20 cm (8") round springform cake tin.

Blitz the biscuits in a food processor to a fine crumb. Transfer to a bowl and stir in the butter, then press the mixture into the base of the prepared cake tin. Use the back of a metal spoon or base of a glass to firmly press the mixture into the tin and ensure it is even. Place in the fridge for 30 minutes to set.

Meanwhile, place the water in a small bowl and sprinkle over the gelatine. Mix until dissolved. Set aside.

In the bowl of a stand mixer with the paddle attachment, beat the cream cheese and sugar until smooth, about 3 minutes. On low speed, add the cream, beating until fully incorporated. Beat in the gelatine mixture.

Pour the cheesecake mixture into the chilled cake tin. Pour the Raspberry Coulis on top and use a butter knife to swirl it through the cheesecake.

Place in the fridge overnight to set. Pile fresh berries on top and dust with icing sugar (optional) before serving.

STORAGE
Store in the fridge for up to 3 days, or freeze for up to 3 months in an airtight container. To thaw, place the cheesecake in the fridge overnight.

Salted Caramel Cheesecake

No-bake cheesecakes deserve all the popularity and praise they get, because they're super easy to make and even easier to eat (addictive even, some might say!). This Salted Caramel Cheesecake is decadent, rich and a little salty – what more could you want from a cheesecake?

SERVES: 8–10
PREPARATION TIME: 15 MINUTES
CHILLING TIME: OVERNIGHT

250 g (9 oz) digestive biscuits
125 g (4½ oz) unsalted butter, melted
4 tablespoons of cold water
3 teaspoons of gelatine powder
1 teaspoon of salt flakes
500 g (1 lb 1oz) Philadelphia cream cheese, room temperature
140 g (5 oz) caster sugar
500 ml (17 fl oz) thickened cream
170 g (6 oz) Salted Caramel Sauce (see page 300)

sea salt flakes, to finish

Grease and line the base of a 20 cm (8") round springform cake tin.

Blitz the biscuits in a food processor to a fine crumb. Stir in the butter and then press the mixture into the base of the prepared cake tin. Use the back of a metal spoon or base of a glass to firmly press the mixture into the tin and ensure it is even. Place in the fridge for 30 minutes to set.

Meanwhile, place the water in a small bowl and sprinkle over the gelatine. Mix until dissolved. Set aside.

In the bowl of a stand mixer with the paddle attachment, beat the cream cheese and sugar until smooth. On low speed, add the cream, beating until fully incorporated. Beat in the gelatine mixture.

Pour the cheesecake mixture into the chilled cake tin. Pour the Salted Caramel Sauce on top and use a butter knife to swirl it through the cheesecake.

Place in the fridge overnight to set. Sprinkle with a pinch of sea salt flakes and serve.

STORAGE
Store in the fridge for up to 3 days, or freeze for up to 3 months in an airtight container. To thaw, place the cheesecake in the fridge overnight.

Baked New York Cheesecake

Nothing screams New York City like a baked New York cheesecake. There are many types of cheesecakes out there, but for me, this recipe is categorically the best. It does take a little more effort than the no-bake variety, but the reward is worth the work.

SERVES: 8–10
PREPARATION TIME: 30 MINUTES
COOKING TIME: 1 HOUR 45 MINUTES
CHILLING TIME: OVERNIGHT

For the base:
225 g (8 oz) digestive biscuits
85 g (3 oz) butter, melted
1 tablespoon of caster sugar
pinch of salt

For the filling:
630 g (1 lb 6 oz) Philadelphia cream cheese
500 g (1 lb 1oz) caster sugar
80 g (2¾ oz) plain flour
8 large eggs, room temperature
1 tablespoon of vanilla extract
500 ml (17 fl oz) thickened cream
380 ml (13 fl oz) sour cream

Preheat the oven to 180°C (400°F). Grease and line the base and sides of a 24 cm (9") round springform cake tin with one large piece of aluminium foil.

Blitz the digestive biscuits in a food processor until crushed to a crumb.

Place the biscuits, melted butter, sugar and salt in a bowl and stir to combine.

Press the crumbs in an even layer onto the base of the prepared cake tin. Bake for 10 minutes. Remove from the oven and allow to cool.

Reduce the oven temperature to 160°C (325°F). Set the kettle to boil.

In the bowl of a stand mixer with the paddle attachment, beat the cream cheese, sugar and flour together on medium speed until smooth, about 2 minutes. Scrape down the sides of the bowl as required.

Add the eggs one at a time, beating until just combined. On low speed, add the vanilla, cream and sour cream, being careful not to over mix.

Pour the cheesecake mix into the cake tin over the biscuit base. Sit the cheesecake in a large roasting pan. Carefully pour boiling water in the roasting pan to come up about 2 cm (¾") of the sides of the cake tin.

Bake for 1 hour and 30 minutes – 1 hour 45 minutes, until lightly golden on top. The baked cheesecake should only wobble a little bit when nudged, as it will continue to cook once it comes out of the oven.

Remove from the oven and cool the cheesecake in the water bath until the water is just warm, about 45 minutes.

Remove the tin from the water bath and then remove the cake from the tin. Cover with plastic wrap and transfer to the fridge to chill overnight before serving.

STORAGE
Store in the fridge for up to 3 days, or freeze for up to 3 months in an airtight container. To thaw, place the cheesecake in the fridge overnight.

BROOKI'S TIP
It really is very important to use a single piece of foil to line your cake tin, as this means no water will get in from the water bath.

Rosemary, Honey and White Chocolate Cheesecake

There are some instances where I know the playful creations popularised at the bakery just won't cut it. At these moments, I turn to the classics, such as this deliciously creamy cheesecake number that tastes like a summer afternoon in Sicily. This cheesecake is something of a rite of passage into the world of adult flavours, with honey as a sweetener and the introduction of rosemary into the biscuit base.

SERVES: 8–10
PREPARATION TIME: 30 MINUTES
CHILLING TIME: OVERNIGHT

For the base:
175 g (6 oz) ginger biscuits
75 g (2½ oz) unsalted butter, melted
1 tablespoon of finely chopped fresh rosemary

For the filling:
400 ml (13½ fl oz) thickened cream
400 g (14 oz) Philadelphia cream cheese,
  room temperature
300 g (10½ oz) white chocolate, melted and
  cooled to room temperature
115 g (4 oz) honey
½ teaspoon of orange extract

fresh figs (optional), rosemary and honey, to serve

Grease and line a 20 cm (8") round springform cake tin.

Blitz the biscuits in a food processor to a fine crumb.

Transfer to a bowl, stir in the butter and rosemary, and mix until combined. Press the mixture into the base of the prepared cake tin. Use the back of a metal spoon or base of a glass to firmly press the mixture into the tin and ensure it is even. Place in the fridge for 30 minutes to set.

In the bowl of a stand mixer with the whisk attachment, whip the cream, cream cheese and melted (room temperature) white chocolate until fully combined. Add half of the honey and the orange extract, beating until just combined.

Pour the cheesecake mixture into the chilled cake tin. Pour over the remaining honey and use a butter knife to swirl through the cheesecake, being careful not to touch the base. Place in the fridge to chill overnight.

Top with fresh figs, if using, rosemary and a drizzle of honey to serve.

STORAGE
Store in the fridge for up to 3 days, or freeze for up to 3 months in an airtight container. To thaw, place the cheesecake in the fridge overnight.

BROOKI'S TIP
To melt the white chocolate, break it into pieces and heat in the microwave in 15-second intervals until just melted. Be careful not to overheat it. Alternatively, you can melt the chocolate over medium-high heat in a bowl over a saucepan of gently simmering water until liquid.

Basque Burnt Cheesecake

While classic cheesecakes are dense and creamy, a Basque-style cheesecake is light and airy – and its unique characteristic is that it is burnt on top. Originating from San Sebastian in the Basque Country in northern Spain, this cheesecake doesn't require a water bath to bake, meaning it's one of the easiest baked cheesecakes to make at home.

SERVES: 8
PREPARATION TIME: 15 MINUTES
COOKING TIME: 45–55 MINUTES
CHILLING TIME: OVERNIGHT

1 kg (2 lb 3 oz) Philadelphia cream cheese, room temperature
400 g (14 oz) caster sugar
200 ml (6½ fl oz) thickened cream
1 teaspoon of vanilla extract
1 tablespoon of flour, sifted
7 large eggs, room temperature

Preheat the oven to 180°C (400°F) and place the shelf in the middle to ensure an even bake.

Line a 20 cm (8") round springform cake tin with one piece of baking paper, roughly pleating the sides against the sides of the tin.

In the bowl of a stand mixer with the paddle attachment, beat the cream cheese for 2 minutes on medium speed. Lower the speed of the mixer and add the sugar, beating just to combine.

Slowly pour in the cream and vanilla. Add the flour and eggs, beating until just combined.

Pour mixture into prepared cake tin, banging on the bench to knock out any air bubbles. Bake for 45–55 minutes, until deep golden on top. Be careful not to overbake, as the cheesecake will continue to cook when cooling. Cool for 10 minutes at room temperature, followed by chilling overnight in the fridge before serving.

STORAGE
Store in the fridge for up to 3 days.

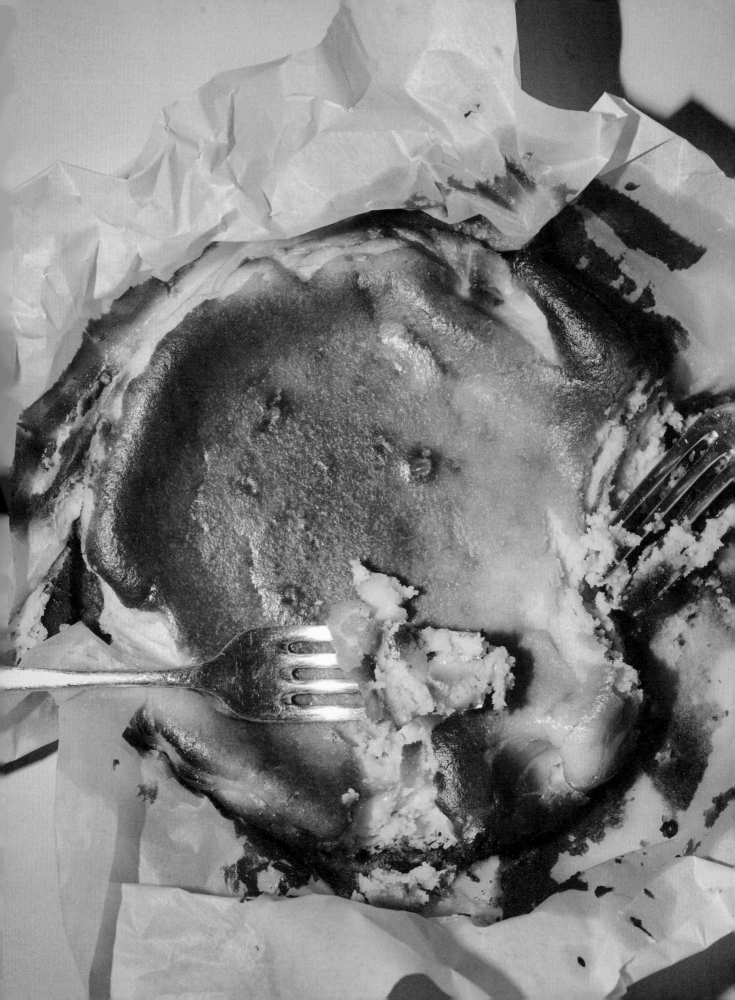

The Ultimate Home of Chocolate: Belgium

When I first ventured to Europe by myself, Belgium was the second country I visited. After landing in Paris in the middle of winter and eating my way around the French capital, I set off for neighbouring Belgium. Until the moment I stepped foot on the platform at Brussels-Central Station, I had very little idea of what to expect. I was in my early twenties after all, and the idea of pitching up in a brand-new city with no hotel reservation and no plans made me giddy with excitement.

It turns out, there's a lot to love about Belgium. For one, chocolate might as well be considered a national food group. With a higher cocoa content than other types of chocolate, Belgian chocolate has the ability to coat your entire mouth in a creamy layer of cocoa goodness. Since discovering Godiva, a chocolatier whose popularity has spread the world over, I was hooked on the taste and texture of Belgian chocolate. Standing in the Bruges market square with my first ever taste in hand, I sipped a mug of dark hot chocolate rich enough to be a dessert, smiling gleefully at the experience of discovering such a treat all by myself and savouring this moment as something only I had the pleasure of being present for. Writing about it now brings back the exact same feelings! It was in these small moments of delight, usually induced by food, that I discovered the world and, in turn, myself. My love for chocolate became a love of learning how to harness its power in baking – as if it were my life's work to understand, not just appreciate, the food I loved so much.

Fast-track to now, and we only use Belgian chocolate in the bakery. That's not to say there aren't some formidable competitors out there (New Zealand has some of the creamiest milk chocolate in the world, for example). But when it comes to baking, the Belgians really know their craft. So if I have any advice when it comes to chocolate, it would be to never scrimp on high-quality chocolate whenever you're baking, as this is one ingredient where the investment really pays off.

Biscoff Cheesecake

When I say my love for Biscoff knows no bounds, I really mean it. This easy no-bake cheesecake is deliciously rich and makes for a great treat to keep sliced up in the freezer, thawing piece by piece as your cravings call for it. The final layer of the cheesecake is pure Biscoff spread. It sets in the fridge to create a luscious layer of smooth caramelised biscuit that matches the base biscuit layer almost too perfectly. It's a real treat!

SERVES: 8–10
PREPARATION TIME: 15 MINUTES
CHILLING TIME: OVERNIGHT

250 g (9 oz) digestive biscuits
125 g (4½ oz) unsalted butter, melted
4 tablespoons of cold water
3 teaspoons of gelatine powder
500 g (1 lb 1oz) Philadelphia cream cheese, room temperature
200 g (7 oz) Biscoff spread
140 g (5 oz) caster sugar
500 ml (17 fl oz) thickened cream

Biscoff biscuits, to garnish (optional)

Grease and line the base of a 20 cm (8") round springform cake tin.

Blitz the biscuits in a food processor to a fine crumb. Transfer to a bowl and stir in the butter, then press the mixture into the base of the prepared cake tin. Use the back of a metal spoon or base of a glass to firmly press the mixture into the tin and ensure it is even. Place in the fridge for 30 minutes to set.

Meanwhile, place the water in a small bowl and sprinkle over the gelatine. Mix until dissolved. Set aside.

In the bowl of a stand mixer with the paddle attachment, beat the cream cheese, 150 g (5¼ oz) Biscoff spread and sugar until smooth, about 3 minutes. On low speed, add the cream, beating until fully incorporated. Beat in the gelatine mixture.

Pour the cheesecake mixture into the chilled cake tin. Pour the remaining Biscoff spread on top (see Brooki's Tip).

Place in the fridge overnight to set. Top with Biscoff biscuits, if using, before serving.

STORAGE
Store in the fridge for up to 3 days, or freeze for up to 3 months in an airtight container. To thaw, place the cheesecake in the fridge overnight.

BROOKI'S TIP
If it's a cool day and the 50 g (1¾ oz) Biscoff spread is too stiff to swirl through the cheesecake, place it in a heatproof bowl and microwave for 20 seconds to liquify.

Lemon Meringue Cheesecake

If you love a tangy lemon pie, then you will love this cheesecake. With a buttery biscuit base, rich citrus curd and the sweetness of meringue, this is a summer specialty worth the extra effort when you dig in. The cheesecake itself can be baked a day ahead, but the meringue is best enjoyed on the same day it is baked (and trust me – there will be no leftovers!).

SERVES: 8–10
PREPARATION TIME: 30 MINUTES
COOKING TIME: 1 HOUR, 10 MINUTES, PLUS 10 MINUTES
CHILLING TIME: 6 HOURS OR OVERNIGHT

For the cheesecake:
250 g (9 oz) digestive biscuits
140 g (5 oz) unsalted butter, melted
500 g (1 lb 1oz) Philadelphia cream cheese, room temperature
300 g (10½ oz) sour cream
155 g (5½ oz) caster sugar
1 tablespoon of lemon zest
2 tablespoons of fresh lemon juice
3 large eggs, room temperature

For the meringue:
3 large egg whites, room temperature
155 g (5½ oz) caster sugar
1 teaspoon of vanilla extract
1 teaspoon of cornflour
½ teaspoon of malt vinegar

Grease and line the base of a 20 cm (8") round springform cake tin.

Blitz the biscuits in a food processor to a fine crumb. Add the butter and mix until fully combined.

Transfer to a bowl and stir in the butter, then press the mixture into the base of the prepared cake tin. Use the back of a metal spoon or base of a glass to firmly press the mixture into the tin and ensure it is even. Place in the fridge for 30 minutes to set.

Preheat the oven to 160°C (350°F).

In the bowl of a stand mixer with the paddle attachment, beat the cream cheese, sour cream, sugar, lemon zest and juice until smooth, about 3 minutes. Add the eggs one at a time and continue beating until well combined.

Pour the cheesecake mixture into the chilled cake tin and bake for 1 hour or until set in the centre. Turn the oven off, leaving the cheesecake inside, with the door slightly ajar for 2 hours. Place in the fridge to chill for at least 6 hours or overnight.

To make the meringue, place the egg whites in the bowl of a stand mixer with the whisk attachment and beat on high speed until firm peaks form, about 5 minutes. Gradually add the sugar, 1 tablespoon at a time, until fully incorporated.

On low speed, add the vanilla, cornflour and vinegar, beating on medium speed until fully combined.

Preheat the oven to 180°C (400°F). Spoon the meringue on top of the cheesecake and spread all over. Bake in the oven for 5–8 minutes or until lightly browned. Place in the fridge to chill for a further 2–3 hours before serving.

STORAGE
This cheesecake is best enjoyed fresh on the day it is made.

Dulce de Leche Cheesecake

I will never forget the first time I discovered dulce de leche. Picture this: a vegetarian in a steak restaurant in downtown Buenos Aires. You'd think I was doomed. To my good fortune, the restaurateur had a stash of freshly baked alfajores in the kitchen and proceeded to feed me a plate of these dulce de leche-filled cookies – for dinner. Since then, my love affair with dulce de leche was sealed and I've never looked back. This cheesecake is rich in taste, but the creamy, thick texture of the dulce de leche is what really sets it apart.

SERVES: 8–10
PREPARATION TIME: 15 MINUTES
CHILLING TIME: OVERNIGHT

250 g (9 oz) digestive biscuits
125 g (4½ oz) unsalted butter, melted
4 tablespoons of cold water
3 teaspoons of gelatine powder
500 g (1 lb 1oz) Philadelphia cream cheese, room temperature
140 g (5 oz) caster sugar
200 g (7 oz) dulce de leche spread
500 ml (17 fl oz) thickened cream

Grease and line the base of a 20 cm (8") round springform cake tin.

Blitz the biscuits in a food processor to a fine crumb. Transfer to a bowl and stir in the butter, then press the mixture into the base of the prepared cake tin. Use the back of a metal spoon or base of a glass to firmly press the mixture into the pan and ensure it is even. Place in the fridge for 30 minutes to set.

Meanwhile, place the water in a small bowl and sprinkle over the gelatine. Mix until dissolved. Set aside.

In the bowl of a stand mixer with the paddle attachment, beat the cream cheese, sugar and 100 g (3½ oz) dulce de leche until smooth, about 3 minutes. On low speed, add the cream, beating until fully incorporated. Beat in the gelatine mixture.

Pour the cheesecake mixture into the chilled cake tin. Pour the remaining 100 g (3½ oz) dulce de leche on top and use a butter knife to swirl through the cheesecake.

Place in the fridge overnight to set before serving.

STORAGE
Store in the fridge for up to 3 days, or freeze for up to 3 months in an airtight container. To thaw, place the cheesecake in the fridge overnight.

Lemon Berry Cheesecake Cups

This recipe was stolen from a dinner party I attended many moons ago, after refusing to leave my friend's home until I had the recipe in hand. Sometimes the best recipes are the simplest, and this is certainly one of those. It is perfect as a finisher to a summer barbecue on a lazy Sunday afternoon.

SERVES: 6
PREPARATION TIME: 15 MINUTES
CHILLING TIME: OVERNIGHT

For the base:
200 g (7 oz) digestive biscuits
85 g (3 oz) unsalted butter, melted
1 tablespoon of caster sugar

For the filling:
325 g (11½ oz) Philadelphia cream cheese,
  room temperature
200 g (7 oz) caster sugar
zest and juice of 2 lemons
½ packet of lemon jelly crystals (40–45 g,
  approx. 1½ oz)
175 ml (5¾ fl oz) hot water (for jelly crystals)
2 teaspoons of powdered gelatine
80 ml (3 fl oz) cold water (for gelatine)
250 ml (8 fl oz) thickened cream, whipped

250 g (9 oz) fresh berries, to serve

Blitz the biscuits in a food processor to a fine crumb. Transfer to a bowl, add the melted butter and sugar, and use your hands to mix. Evenly distribute the crumbs between six glasses and place in the fridge to chill.

Meanwhile, make the cheesecake by placing the cream cheese in the bowl of a stand mixer with the paddle attachment. Beat for 3 minutes, scraping down the sides of the bowl as needed.

Add the sugar and beat for a further 3 minutes.

Turn the mixer to low speed and add the lemon zest and juice.

Place the jelly crystals in a small bowl and add hot water. Mix until dissolved and allow to cool. Pour the dissolved jelly into the cream cheese mixture and beat to combine.

Place 80 ml (3 fl oz) water in a small bowl and sprinkle over the gelatine. Use a fork to whisk until fully incorporated. Set aside for 5 minutes, or until spongy. Pour into the filling mixture and beat on low speed until fully incorporated.

Lastly, fold in the whipped cream and pour the mixture evenly between the glasses. Chill for at least 4 hours or overnight. Once set, top with fresh berries to serve.

STORAGE
You can make these 1 day in advance if kept refrigerated, and then decorate with the fresh berries just before serving.

Chai Latte Cheesecake

As far as cheesecakes go, this is one of the more surprising options in the bakery, but every customer who chooses to try the Chai Latte Cheesecake loves it. This dessert is particularly good when the weather is cooling off and we start to crave those winter comforts. And if you like some spice in your baking, this is definitely the one for you.

SERVES: 8–10
PREPARATION TIME: 15 MINUTES
CHILLING TIME: 4 HOURS OR OVERNIGHT

For the base:
200 g (7 oz) digestive biscuits
70 g (2½ oz) pecans
½ teaspoon of ground ginger
½ teaspoon of ground cinnamon
125 g (4½ oz) unsalted butter, melted

For the cheesecake:
4 tablespoons of cold water
3 teaspoons of gelatine powder
500 g (1 lb 1oz) Philadelphia cream cheese, room temperature
140 g (5 oz) caster sugar
500 ml (17 fl oz) thickened cream
1 teaspoon of ground ginger
1 teaspoon of ground nutmeg
1 teaspoon of ground cinnamon
¼ teaspoon of ground cloves
¼ teaspoon of ground cardamom

For the cinnamon sugar dusting:
2 teaspoons of caster sugar
2 teaspoons of ground cinnamon

Grease and line the base of a 20 cm (8") round springform cake tin.

Blitz the biscuits and pecans in a food processor to a fine crumb. Transfer to a bowl and stir in the ginger, cinnamon and melted butter, mixing to combine. Press the mixture into the base of the prepared cake tin. Use the back of a metal spoon or base of a glass to firmly press the mixture into the pan and ensure it is even. Place in the fridge for 30 minutes to set.

Meanwhile, place the water in a small bowl and sprinkle over the gelatine. Mix until dissolved. Set aside.

In the bowl of a stand mixer with the paddle attachment, beat the cream cheese and sugar until smooth, about 3 minutes. On low speed, add the cream, beating until fully incorporated. Beat in the gelatine mixture. On low speed, beat in the ginger, nutmeg, cinnamon, cloves and cardamom, mixing until just combined.

Pour the cheesecake mixture into the chilled cake tin and place in the fridge for 4 hours, or overnight, to set.

Combine the sugar and cinnamon in a small bowl to make the cinnamon sugar dusting, and sprinkle over the top of the cheesecake just before serving.

STORAGE
Store in the fridge for up to 3 days, or freeze for up to 3 months in an airtight container. To thaw, place the cheesecake in the fridge overnight.

SLICES

Slices got a lot of love in my childhood household and, if you ask me, it was well-deserved. My parents both grew up in a small town at the far northwest point of the island of Tasmania, where country baking is not just a beloved pastime, but a sport (truly, there are many bake fairs and local competitions throughout the year). Because of this, my mum is an expert when it comes to country cooking, especially slice recipes. When I was a kid, there'd always be one in our fridge. There was never a shortage of Tupperware containers half-filled with homemade treats, ready to serve to a roster of guests who would pass through on weekends. When I set out to write this book I never imagined there would be an entire chapter devoted to slices, but I would be remiss not to include the recipes that defined my childhood. If you're yet to discover the sheer brilliance of no-bake baking, consider this chapter your safe space for exploration. These recipes are some of the easiest to follow, and yet often yield the tastiest creations that leave your friends begging for the recipe.

Raspberry Coconut Slice

A classic. An icon. My mum wouldn't let me publish a cookbook with my name on it without including her beloved Raspberry Coconut Slice (and rightly so – it's a good 'un). This slice recipe has been passed down through our family for generations and I hope you can do the same.

SERVES: 16
PREPARATION TIME: 15 MINUTES
COOKING TIME: 45 MINUTES
COOLING TIME: 2 HOURS

For the base:
300 g (10½ oz) plain flour
110 g (3¾ oz) caster sugar
125 g (4½ oz) unsalted butter, chilled and cubed
1 large egg, room temperature
1 teaspoon of vanilla extract
225 g (8 oz) raspberry jam

For the topping:
2 egg whites
110 g (3¾ oz) caster sugar
85 g (3 oz) unsweetened desiccated coconut
80 g (2¾ oz) shredded coconut

To make the base:

Preheat the oven to 180°C (400°F). Grease and line a 20 cm (8") square baking tin with baking paper, ensuring two sides overhang for easy removal.

Place the flour, caster sugar and butter into a food processor and blend until the mix resembles breadcrumbs.

Add the egg and vanilla, and process until the mixture forms a dough.

Transfer the dough to the prepared baking tin and use the back of a metal spoon or base of a glass to firmly press down and ensure it is even.

Bake for 15–20 minutes, or until the top begins to turn golden.

Spread the jam evenly over the warm base and set aside to cool.

To make the topping:

In the bowl of a stand mixer with the whisk attachment, whisk the egg whites and caster sugar together until soft peaks form.

On low speed, add the desiccated and shredded coconut, and whisk until combined. Spread the mixture over the jam.

Bake for 25 minutes, or until the coconut on top begins to turn golden.

Allow the slice to cool completely in the tin before slicing.

STORAGE
Store at room temperature in an airtight container for up to 5 days, out of direct sunlight.

Caramel Slice

Caramel slice was a staple baked treat in our household when I was growing up, and because it was my mum's favourite, it became my favourite too. The secret to caramel slice, I have found, is to have a generous ratio of caramel filling to base, so that it melts away in your mouth in every bite. I owe a lot of this chapter to my mum, who always made sure there was a homemade slice in the fridge.

SERVES: 16
PREPARATION TIME: 15 MINUTES
CHILLING TIME: 2 HOURS

For the base:
150 g (5¼ oz) plain flour
80 g (2¾ oz) light brown sugar
45 g (1½ oz) unsweetened desiccated coconut
125 g (4½ oz) unsalted butter, melted

For the caramel layer:
125 g (4½ oz) unsalted butter, chilled and cubed
80 g (2¾ oz) light brown sugar
1 teaspoon of vanilla extract
395 g (14 oz) can sweetened condensed milk

For the chocolate layer:
200 g (7 oz) milk chocolate, broken into pieces
1 tablespoon of vegetable oil

To make the base:

Preheat the oven to 180°C (400°F). Grease and line a 33 × 23 cm (13 × 9") rectangular tin with baking paper, ensuring two sides overhang for easy removal.

In a bowl, mix the base ingredients together with your hands and transfer to the prepared tin. Use the back of a metal spoon or base of a glass to firmly press the mixture down and ensure it is even.

Bake for 15 minutes until the top is golden. Remove from the oven.

To make the caramel layer:

Reduce the oven temperature to 160°C (350°F).

Place the butter, sugar and vanilla in a saucepan over medium heat. Stir continuously until the mixture starts to simmer.

Pour in the condensed milk and whisk continuously for 5 minutes. Once bubbles start to appear, whisk vigorously for 1 minute before removing from the heat and pouring over the base.

Bake for 12 minutes. Remove from the oven and allow to cool for 20 minutes at room temperature before placing in the fridge to chill for 30 minutes.

To make the chocolate layer:

Place the chocolate and oil in a microwave-safe bowl. Microwave in 30-second intervals, stirring in between, until the chocolate fully melts.

Pour the chocolate over the caramel and spread evenly with a spatula. Tap the pan gently on the bench and give it a little shake to ensure the chocolate is evenly distributed.

Refrigerate for 2 hours. Once set, slice and enjoy!

STORAGE
Store in an airtight container in the fridge for up to 7 days.

CUSTOMISATION
One of my favourite ways to customise Caramel Slice is to sprinkle caramelised cornflakes over the top of the chocolate layer before placing it in the fridge to set. It provides an extra crunch and is a delicious tip to keep in your repertoire to spruce up any tray bake.

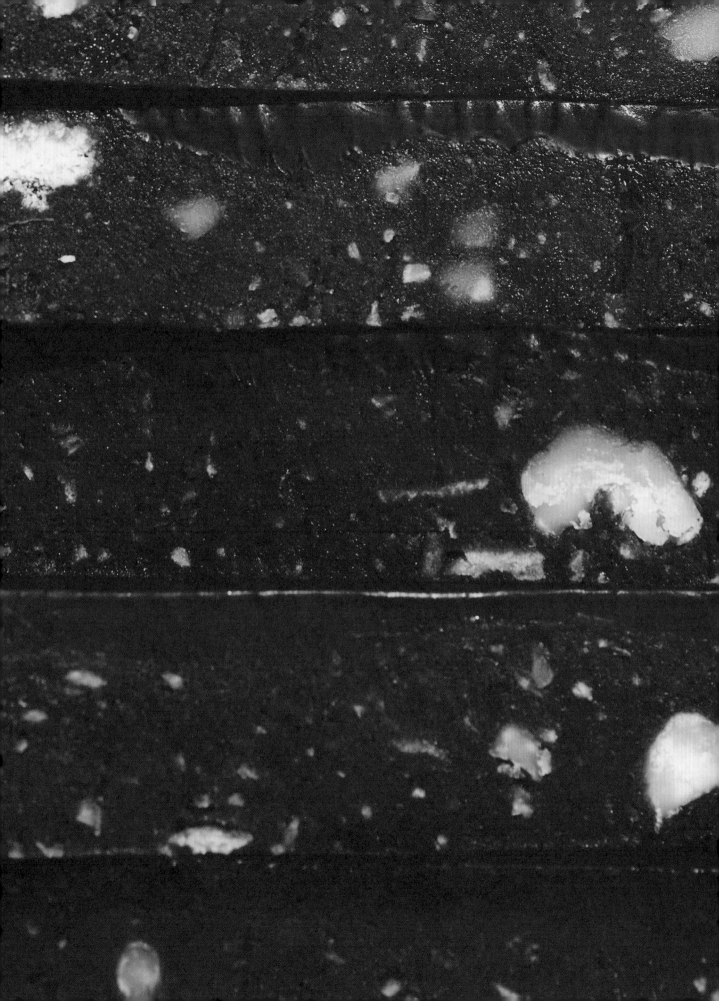

Hedgehog Slice

Sometimes, you just feel like a classic. This Hedgehog Slice, with its biscuity crunch, is a retro classic – and so easy to make. Don't overlook it.

SERVES: 16
PREPARATION TIME: 15 MINUTES
CHILLING TIME: 3 HOURS

For the base:
250 g (9 oz) plain sweet biscuits (I use Arnott's Marie)
100 g (3½ oz) unsalted butter
395 g (14 oz) can sweetened condensed milk
150 g (5¼ oz) dark chocolate, broken into pieces
50 g (1¾ oz) unsweetened desiccated coconut
65 g (2¼ oz) walnuts, roughly chopped
2 tablespoons of cocoa powder

For the chocolate topping:
290 g (10¼ oz) dark chocolate, broken into pieces
2 tablespoons of vegetable oil

To make the base:

Grease and line a 24 × 15.5 cm (9½ × 6") rectangular slice tin with baking paper, ensuring two sides overhang for easy removal.

Blitz the biscuits in a food processor to a fine crumb.

Place the butter, sweetened condensed milk and dark chocolate into a microwave-safe bowl and heat in 30-second intervals for around 3–4 minutes, or until melted, stirring in between.

Add the crushed biscuits, coconut, walnuts and cocoa powder, and mix together.

Transfer the mixture to the prepared tin and use the back of a metal spoon or base of a glass to firmly press the mixture down and ensure it is even.

To make the chocolate topping:

Melt the dark chocolate and vegetable oil in a microwave-safe bowl, stirring every 30 seconds, until melted.

Pour the melted chocolate over the top of the slice and refrigerate for a minimum of 3 hours to set before slicing.

STORAGE
Store in an airtight container in the fridge for up to 7 days.
Alternatively, you can freeze this slice for up to 2 months.

Jelly Slice

My mum is the best baker I know. When I signed the deal to write this cookbook, she was the first person I called to share the news. Almost instantly, my messages were flooded with her best baking recipes, providing me with a walk down memory lane.

Although there is nothing particularly fancy about a jelly slice, I have it on good authority this is the best recipe out there. So, if you fancy making a quick and easy slice to take to a friend's house (or to tuck into yourself), this is the perfect afternoon-tea snack.

SERVES: 12
PREPARATION TIME: 15 MINUTES
CHILLING TIME: 3 HOURS + OVERNIGHT

85 g (3 oz) packet red jelly crystals
250 g (9 oz) Arnott's milk arrowroot biscuits
170 g (6 oz) unsalted butter, melted
395 g (14 oz) can sweetened condensed milk
juice of 1 lemon
4 tablespoons of cold water
3 teaspoons of gelatine

Prepare jelly according to the packet instructions and set aside to cool at room temperature.

Grease and line a 24 × 15.5 cm (9½ × 6") rectangular baking tin with baking paper, ensuring two sides overhang for easy removal.

Blitz the biscuits in a food processor to a fine crumb. Pour over the melted butter and mix until combined. Transfer the biscuit base into the prepared tin and use the back of a metal spoon or base of a glass to firmly press the mixture down and ensure it is even. Refrigerate to set, about 2 hours.

Meanwhile, place the water in a small bowl and sprinkle over the gelatine. Mix until dissolved. Set aside.

In a separate bowl, mix the condensed milk with the lemon juice. Add the gelatine mixture and whisk until completely combined.

Pour the mixture over the biscuit base and place in the fridge to set, around 1 hour.

Gently pour the cooled jelly over the top of the slice and refrigerate for 5 hours or overnight. Slice once set.

STORAGE
Store in an airtight container in the fridge for up to 3 days.

Rice Crispy Choc Peanut Butter Fudge Slice

To my surprise, this fudge slice has been a bestseller in the bakery since we opened. It is rich in peanut butter, and the rice crispy crunch texture is what keeps people coming back for more. Best of all, it's one of the easiest treats to make and requires no baking.

SERVES: 16
PREPARATION TIME: 15 MINUTES
CHILLING TIME: 2 HOURS

For the base layer:
700 g (1lb 8½ oz) white chocolate, roughly chopped
560 g (1lb 3¾ oz) smooth peanut butter
50 g (1¾ oz) rice bubbles

For the top layer:
545 g (1 lb 3 oz) milk chocolate
840 g (1 lb 13 oz) smooth peanut butter
30 g unsalted butter
75 g (2½ oz) rice bubbles

To make the base layer:

Grease and line a 33 × 23 cm (13 × 9") rectangular baking tin with baking paper, ensuring two sides overhang for easy removal.

Place the chocolate and peanut butter in a microwave-safe bowl. Heat in 30-second intervals until the mixture is melted completely.

Add the rice bubbles and mix until combined.

Transfer the mixture into the prepared tin, using a spatula to press down evenly.

Place in the freezer to set for 20 minutes.

To make the top layer:

Place the chocolate, peanut butter and butter in a microwave-safe bowl and heat in 30-second intervals until melted and smooth.

Add the rice bubbles and mix until combined.

Place the top layer over the base, using a spatula to press down evenly, and refrigerate for 2 hours before slicing.

STORAGE
Store in an airtight container in the fridge for up to 1 week.

Vegan Choc Peanut Butter Fudge Slice (V)

I'm not a vegan (I could never quit butter), but I almost always choose to take home a piece of this vegan fudge slice on my way out of the bakery. It is super easy to make and a great choice for dietary restrictions, as it contains no dairy, eggs or gluten. It's up to you if you use crunchy or smooth peanut butter (there's a debate I don't wish to enter!). But for me, it's smooth peanut butter all day, every day.

SERVES: 16
PREPARATION TIME: 15 MINUTES
CHILLING TIME: 2 HOURS

For the base:
260 g (9 oz) peanut butter
120 ml (4 fl oz) maple syrup
110 g (3¾ oz) coconut flour

For the chocolate layer:
100 g (3½ oz) vegan dark chocolate, broken into pieces
65 g (2¼ oz) peanut butter
2 tablespoons of coconut oil

To make the base:

Line a 24 cm (9") square tin with baking paper, ensuring two sides overhang for easy removal.

In a bowl, stir the peanut butter and maple syrup together to create a paste.

Stir in the coconut flour and use your hands to knead the dough into a ball.

Place the dough into the prepared tin. Use the back of a metal spoon to firmly press the mixture down and ensure it is even.

Place in the freezer for 20 minutes to set, while you prepare the chocolate layer.

To make the chocolate layer:

Place the chocolate, peanut butter and coconut oil in a microwave-safe bowl and heat in 30-second intervals until completely melted.

Pour the chocolate layer over the base and spread evenly with a spatula.

Return to the freezer to set for 15 minutes. Slice into 16 pieces.

STORAGE
Store in an airtight container in the fridge for up to 7 days.
Alternatively, you can freeze this slice for up to 2 months.

Honey Almond Slice

The crunchy golden almonds on top of this slice make it taste fancier than it is. Incredibly moreish, it's best with an afternoon cup of tea or coffee. And it is one of the easiest things you'll ever bake!

SERVES: 16
PREPARATION TIME: 10 MINUTES
COOKING TIME: 27 MINUTES
COOLING TIME: 2 HOURS

For the base:
100 g (3½ oz) unsalted butter
60 g (2 oz) light brown sugar
115 g (4 oz) plain flour
60 g (2 oz) almond meal

For the topping:
80 g (2¾ oz) unsalted butter
60 g (2 oz) honey
85 g (3 oz) flaked almonds

Preheat the oven to 170°C (375°F). Grease and line a 20 cm (8") square baking tin with baking paper, ensuring two sides overhang for easy removal.

Place the butter in a large microwave-safe bowl and heat in 20-second intervals until melted.

Add the sugar, flour and almond meal to the melted butter and mix with a wooden spoon until combined.

Place the mixture into the prepared tin and use the back of a metal spoon or base of a glass to firmly press down and ensure it is even.

Bake for 12 minutes until lightly golden.

Meanwhile, heat the butter and honey for the topping in a microwave-safe bowl until melted. Stir the flaked almonds through the mixture and spread over the base.

Bake for a further 15 minutes until lightly golden. Remove from the oven and allow to cool completely before slicing.

STORAGE
Store in an airtight container in the fridge for up to 1 week.
Alternatively, you can freeze this slice for up to 3 months.

Lemon Slice

This is a super easy slice to make, but its popularity should not be underestimated. If you find yourself in need of a quick baked treat for tomorrow's morning tea, you can whip this one up before bed. All you need to do the following day is cut up the slice and resist the temptation to eat it all on your way to work!

SERVES: 16
PREPARATION TIME: 15 MINUTES
CHILLING TIME: 4 HOURS

For the base:
250 g (9 oz) plain sweet biscuits (I use Arnott's Marie biscuits)
90 g (3 oz) unsweetened desiccated coconut
zest and juice of 1 lemon
80 g (2¾ oz) unsalted butter, melted
250 g (9 oz) sweetened condensed milk

For the lemon frosting:
360 g (12¾ oz) icing sugar
90 g (3 oz) unsalted butter, room temperature
75 ml (2½ fl oz) lemon juice
20 g (¾ oz) unsweetened desiccated coconut, to decorate

To make the base:

Grease and line a 24 × 15.5 cm (9½ × 6") rectangular slice tin with baking paper, ensuring two sides overhang for easy removal.

Blitz the biscuits in a food processor to a fine crumb then transfer to a bowl. Add the desiccated coconut and lemon zest. Mix to combine.

Add the lemon juice, melted butter and condensed milk. Mix until well combined.

Transfer the biscuit base into the prepared tin, and use the back of a metal spoon or base of a glass to firmly press the mixture down and ensure it is even. Place in the fridge to set.

To make the lemon frosting:

In the bowl of a stand mixer with the whisk attachment, whisk the icing sugar, butter and lemon juice on medium speed until creamy. If the frosting is too thick to spread, add a little more lemon juice.

Spread the frosting over the cooled biscuit base, sprinkling some extra coconut on top to decorate. Place in the fridge to set completely before slicing.

STORAGE
Store in an airtight container in the fridge for up to 7 days.
Alternatively, you can freeze this slice for up to 2 months.

MACARONS

Macarons were the first pastry I fell in love with. It started back in my travel days when I was running around Paris in search of the best salted caramel macaron (you'll find them at Carette). After converting euros to dollars and realising just how much I was spending on each bite, I decided to learn how to make them for myself. A quick internet search later and I discovered I could attend a day class right there in Paris, learning to make these delicate creations from scratch. By the time I returned home to Australia, I was eating bucketloads of macarons for breakfast. While they might be known as one of the most difficult pastries to master, I promise you that once you've tried the method I suggest here, you'll be making professional-looking macarons in no time.

Tiramisu Macarons

In case you hadn't already noticed, I really love tiramisu (perhaps unsurprising given my affinity to coffee). Not just as a post-dinner dessert, but as a flavour I can re-create in various forms so I can enjoy it throughout the day, with these macarons being one of them. They are the perfect balance of rich and creamy, finished off with a generous dusting of cocoa powder over the shells.

MAKES: 50 SHELLS (25 MACARONS)
PREPARATION TIME: 20 MINUTES
COOKING TIME: 12 MINUTES
COOLING TIME: 20 MINUTES

For the macaron shells:
ALMOND PASTE:
100 g (3½ oz) icing sugar, sifted
100 g (3½ oz) almond meal, sifted
36 g (1¼ oz) egg whites, room temperature
1 teaspoon of brown food colouring gel
MERINGUE:
36 g (1¼ oz) egg whites, room temperature
100 g (3½ oz) caster sugar
25 ml (2 teaspoons) water

For the tiramisu filling:
60 g (2 oz) unsalted butter, room temperature
115 g (4 oz) mascarpone cheese, room temperature
240 g (8½ oz) icing sugar, sifted
2 tablespoons of coffee liqueur

cocoa powder, to dust

To make the macaron shells:

Measure all ingredients before starting. Place a piping bag fitted with a round 2A piping tip in a milkshake cup or tall glass to support it when filling the bag. Place macaron-stencilled silicon mats on baking trays.

Sift icing sugar and almond meal into a bowl, discarding any chunks that don't easily pass through the sieve. Add 36 g (1¼ oz) egg whites to create an almond paste. Mix until combined, being careful not to over mix. Add the gel food colouring and mix until just combined. Set aside.

Place the remaining 36 g (1¼ oz) egg whites in the bowl of a stand mixer with the whisk attachment.

Meanwhile, place the caster sugar and water in a saucepan with your sugar thermometer. Heat the sugar to 112°C (234°F). Once temperature is reached, turn the mixer on to low and whisk the egg whites, before gradually turning up the speed to the highest setting. Once the sugar syrup reaches 118°C (244°F), remove from the heat and turn the mixer down to a low-medium setting. Slowly and carefully pour the sugar mixture into the egg whites, aiming to pour between the side of the bowl and the whisk attachment. Once all the sugar is poured in, turn the mixer back to the highest setting to make an Italian meringue.

Whisk until the bowl is cool to the touch.

Fold one-third of the meringue into the almond paste at a time until the mixture forms a ribbon. Transfer the mixture into your prepared piping bag and pipe 50 macaron shells onto the mats.

Tap the baking trays lightly on the bench to knock out any air bubbles.

Leave the macarons to sit at room temperature for at least 30 minutes, to form a skin. At this time, preheat the oven to 160°C (350°F) and when ready, bake the macarons for 12 minutes, opening the door very briefly halfway through to release excess steam.

Once the macarons have baked, allow them to cool completely before flipping half of them over so the flat surface is facing upwards. In the meantime, prepare the tiramisu filling.

→

To make the tiramisu filling:

In the bowl of a stand mixer with the paddle attachment, cream together the butter and mascarpone cheese until smooth.

Add the sifted icing sugar and beat on low until combined.

Add the coffee liqueur and beat for a further 2 minutes on high speed until glossy.

To assemble, pipe the tiramisu filling onto the flat base of half of the macaron shells, then lightly push an uniced shell on top to sandwich the shells together. Dust with cocoa powder before placing in the fridge to set.

STORAGE
Assembled macarons will keep for up to 7 days refrigerated, just be sure to leave them at room temperature for 30 minutes before eating as they are best enjoyed at room temperature. Assembled macarons can be frozen on the same day you bake them, for up to 1 month. To thaw, place the macarons in the fridge for at least 1 hour with plastic wrap over the container to capture any condensation.

Oreo Cheesecake Macarons

This macaron is one of the most popular in the bakery, which is perhaps no surprise! Cookies and cream has always been a combination loved by many, but the addition of cream cheese makes these macarons taste like an Oreo cheesecake in just one bite – what's there not to love?

MAKES: 50 SHELLS (25 MACARONS)
PREPARATION TIME: 20 MINUTES
COOKING TIME: 12 MINUTES
COOLING TIME: 20 MINUTES

For the macaron shells:
ALMOND PASTE:
100 g (3½ oz) icing sugar, sifted
100 g (3½ oz) almond meal, sifted
36 g (1¼ oz) egg whites, room temperature
1 teaspoon of sky-blue food colouring gel
MERINGUE:
36 g (1¼ oz) egg whites, room temperature
100 g (3½ oz) caster sugar
25 ml (2 teaspoons) water

5 Oreo cookies, blitzed to a fine crumb

For the cream cheese filling:
60 g (2 oz) butter, room temperature and cubed
100 g (3½ oz) Philadelphia cream cheese,
 room temperature
200 g (7 oz) icing sugar, sifted

5 Oreo cookies, blitzed to a fine crumb

To make the macaron shells:

Measure all ingredients before starting. Place a piping bag fitted with a round 2A piping tip in a milkshake cup or tall glass to support it when filling the bag. Place macaron-stencilled silicon mats on baking trays.

Sift icing sugar and almond meal into a bowl, discarding any chunks that don't easily pass through the sieve. Add 36 g (1¼ oz) egg whites to create an almond paste. Mix until combined, being careful not to over mix. Add the gel food colouring and mix until just combined. Set aside.

Place the remaining 36 g (1¼ oz) egg whites in the bowl of a stand mixer with the whisk attachment.

Meanwhile, place the caster sugar and water in a saucepan with your sugar thermometer. Heat the sugar to 112°C (234°F). Once temperature is reached, turn the mixer on to low and whisk the egg whites, before gradually turning up the speed to the highest setting. Once the sugar syrup reaches 118°C (244°F), remove from the heat and turn the mixer down to a low-medium setting. Slowly and carefully pour the sugar mixture into the egg whites, aiming to pour between the side of the bowl and the whisk attachment. Once all the sugar is poured in, turn the mixer back to the highest setting to make an Italian meringue.

Whisk until the bowl is cool to the touch.

Fold one-third of the meringue into the almond paste at a time until the mixture forms a ribbon. Transfer the mixture into your prepared piping bag and pipe 50 macaron shells onto the mats.

Tap the baking trays gently on the bench to knock out any air bubbles.

Sprinkle some Oreo crumbs over the shells.

Leave the macarons to sit at room temperature for at least 30 minutes to form a skin. At this time, preheat the oven to 160°C (350°F) and when ready, bake the macarons for 12 minutes, opening the door very briefly halfway through to release excess steam.

Once the macarons have baked, allow them to cool completely before flipping half of them over so the flat surface is facing upwards. In the meantime, prepare the cream cheese filling.

To make the cream cheese filling:

Place the butter in the bowl of a stand mixer with the paddle attachment and beat on high speed for 5 minutes, scraping down the sides of the bowl as required.

Once the butter is glossy and pale in colour, add the cream cheese and continue to beat for 3 minutes.

Turn the speed to low and add the sifted icing sugar. Beat for 5 minutes.

Finally, add the Oreo crumbs to the mixture and beat on low speed until just combined.

To assemble, pipe the buttercream filling onto the flat base of half of the macaron shells, then lightly push an uniced shell on top to sandwich the shells together.

STORAGE
Assembled macarons will keep for up to 7 days refrigerated, just be sure to leave them at room temperature for 30 minutes before eating as they are best enjoyed at room temperature. Assembled macarons can be frozen on the same day you bake them, for up to 1 month. To thaw, place the macarons in the fridge for at least 1 hour with plastic wrap over the container to capture any condensation.

Biscoff Macarons

The secret to creating great macaron flavours is to ensure each bite packs a punch. These Biscoff macarons are my personal favourite filling, as the Biscoff ganache is intense and deliciously creamy.

MAKES: 50 SHELLS (25 MACARONS)
PREPARATION TIME: 20 MINUTES
COOKING TIME: 12 MINUTES
COOLING TIME: 20 MINUTES

For the Biscoff ganache filling:
120 g (4¼ oz) white chocolate, broken into pieces
80 g (2¾ oz) Biscoff spread
20 g (¾ oz) unsalted butter
120 ml (4 fl oz) thickened cream

For the macaron shells:
ALMOND PASTE:
100 g (3½ oz) icing sugar, sifted
100 g (3½ oz) almond meal, sifted
36 g (1¼ oz) egg whites, room temperature
MERINGUE:
36 g (1¼ oz) egg whites, room temperature
100 g (3½ oz) caster sugar
25 ml (2 teaspoons) water

STORAGE
Assembled macarons will keep for up to 7 days refrigerated, just be sure to leave them at room temperature for 30 minutes before eating as they are best enjoyed at room temperature. Assembled macarons can be frozen on the same day you bake them, for up to 1 month. To thaw, place the macarons in the fridge for at least 1 hour with plastic wrap over the container to capture any condensation.

To make the Biscoff ganache filling:

The ganache requires about 2 hours to set, so I recommend making this first. You can make the ganache up to a week in advance and store it in the fridge – just be sure to allow it to come to room temperature before using.

Place chocolate, Biscoff spread and butter in a heatproof bowl and set aside.

Place cream in a microwave-safe bowl and microwave for 15-second intervals until it just begins to bubble (about 45 seconds). Alternatively, you can heat the cream over medium-high heat in a saucepan until it starts to boil.

Pour the cream over the chocolate, Biscoff spread and butter. Leave to sit for a few minutes.

Use a stick blender (or a spoon if you don't have one) to mix the ganache until the mixture becomes smooth and glossy.

Press a piece of plastic wrap on top of the ganache to prevent a skin from forming. Place in the fridge to chill for about 2 hours.

To make the macaron shells:

Measure all ingredients before starting. Place a piping bag fitted with a round 2A piping tip in a milkshake cup or tall glass to support it when filling the bag. Place macaron-stencilled silicon mats on baking trays.

Sift icing sugar and almond meal into a bowl, discarding any chunks that don't easily pass through the sieve. Add 36 g (1¼ oz) egg whites to create an almond paste. Mix until combined, being careful not to over mix. Set aside.

Place the remaining 36 g (1¼ oz) egg whites in the bowl of a stand mixer with the whisk attachment.

Meanwhile, place the caster sugar and water in a saucepan with your sugar thermometer. Heat the sugar to 112°C (234°F). Once temperature is reached, turn the mixer on to low and whisk the egg whites, before gradually turning up the speed to the highest setting. Once the sugar syrup reaches 118°C (244°F), remove from the heat and turn the mixer down to a low-medium setting. Slowly and carefully pour the sugar mixture into the egg whites, aiming to pour between the side of the bowl and the whisk attachment. Once all the sugar is poured in, turn the mixer back to the highest setting to make an Italian meringue.

Whisk until the bowl is cool to the touch.

Fold one-third of the meringue into the almond paste at a time until the mixture forms a ribbon. Transfer the mixture into your prepared piping bag and pipe 50 macaron shells onto the mats.

Tap the baking trays gently on the bench to knock out any air bubbles.

Leave the macarons to sit at room temperature for at least 30 minutes, to form a skin. At this time, preheat the oven to 160°C (350°F) and when ready, bake the macarons for 12 minutes, opening the door very briefly halfway through to release excess steam.

Once the macarons have baked, allow them to cool completely before flipping half of them over so the flat surface is facing upwards.

To assemble, pipe the ganache filling onto the flat base of half of the macaron shells, then lightly push an uniced shell on top to sandwich the shells together.

Red Velvet Macarons

Red velvet has become one of the most popular styles in the bakery – whether it is in the form of a cookie, a brownie, a cupcake or a macaron.

The flavour is deliciously well balanced, especially when matched with a luscious cream cheese filling.

MAKES: 50 SHELLS (25 MACARONS)
PREPARATION TIME: 20 MINUTES
COOKING TIME: 12 MINUTES
COOLING TIME: 20 MINUTES

For the macaron shells:
ALMOND PASTE:
100 g (3½ oz) icing sugar, sifted
100 g (3½ oz) almond meal, sifted
36 g (1¼ oz) egg whites, room temperature
1 teaspoon of red food colouring gel
MERINGUE:
36 g (1¼ oz) egg whites, room temperature
100 g (3½ oz) caster sugar
25 ml (2 teaspoons) water

For the cream cheese filling:
60 g (2 oz) unsalted butter,
  room temperature and cubed
100 g (3½ oz) Philadelphia cream cheese,
  room temperature
200 g (7 oz) icing sugar, sifted
1 teaspoon of red velvet flavouring (optional)

To make the macaron shells:

Measure all ingredients before starting. Place a piping bag fitted with a round 2A piping tip in a milkshake cup or tall glass to support it when filling the bag. Place macaron-stencilled silicon mats on baking trays.

Sift icing sugar and almond meal into a bowl, discarding any chunks that don't easily pass through the sieve. Add 36 g (1¼ oz) egg whites to create an almond paste. Mix until combined, being careful not to over mix. Add the gel food colouring and mix until just combined. Set aside.

Place the remaining 36 g (1¼ oz) egg whites in another stand mixer bowl with the whisk attachment.

Meanwhile, place the caster sugar and water in a saucepan with your sugar thermometer. Heat the sugar to 112°C (234°F). Once temperature is reached, turn the mixer on to low and whisk the egg whites, before gradually turning up the speed to the highest setting. Once the sugar syrup reaches 118°C (244°F), remove from the heat and turn the mixer down to a low-medium setting. Slowly and carefully pour the sugar mixture into the egg whites, aiming to pour between the side of the bowl and the whisk attachment. Once all the sugar is poured in, turn the mixer back to the highest setting to make an Italian meringue.

Whisk until the bowl is cool to the touch.

Fold one-third of the meringue into the almond paste at a time until the mixture forms a ribbon. Transfer the mixture into your prepared piping bag and pipe 50 macaron shells onto the mats.

Tap the baking trays lightly on the bench to knock out any air bubbles.

Leave the macarons to sit at room temperature for at least 30 minutes, to form a skin. At this time, preheat the oven to 160°C (350°F) and when ready, bake the macarons for 12 minutes, opening the door very briefly halfway through to release excess steam.

Once the macarons have baked, allow them to cool completely before flipping half of them over so the flat surface is facing upwards. In the meantime, prepare the cream cheese filling.

STORAGE
Assembled macarons will keep for up to 7 days refrigerated, just be sure to leave them at room temperature for 30 minutes before eating as they are best enjoyed at room temperature. Assembled macarons can be frozen on the same day you bake them, for up to 1 month. To thaw, place the macarons in the fridge for at least 1 hour with plastic wrap over the container to capture any condensation.

To make the cream cheese filling:

Place the butter in the bowl of a stand mixer with the paddle attachment and beat for 3–5 minutes, scraping down the sides of the bowl as required.

Once the butter is glossy and pale in colour, turn the speed to low and add the cream cheese. Beat for a further 3–5 minutes.

Turn the mixer to the lowest setting and slowly add the sifted icing sugar. Beat for a further 5–10 minutes until light and fluffy.

Add the flavouring (if using), and beat until combined.

To assemble, pipe the cream cheese filling onto the flat base of half of the macaron shells, then lightly push an uniced shell on top to sandwich the shells together.

Birthday Cake Macarons

These birthday cake macarons are my favourite gift to give friends on their special day – they are delicate and delicious, and also look quite impressive!

You will find cake batter flavouring at your local cake store and online – and believe me when I say the flavour packs a punch!

MAKES: 50 SHELLS (25 MACARONS)
PREPARATION TIME: 20 MINUTES
COOKING TIME: 12 MINUTES
COOLING TIME: 20 MINUTES

For the macaron shells:
ALMOND PASTE:
100 g (3½ oz) icing sugar, sifted
100 g (3½ oz) almond meal, sifted
36 g (1¼ oz) egg whites, room temperature
MERINGUE:
36g (1¼ oz) egg whites, room temperature
100 g (3½ oz) caster sugar
25 ml (2 teaspoons) water
DECORATION
50 g (1¾ oz) 100s and 1000s rainbow nonpareils

For the buttercream filling:
125 g (4½ oz) unsalted butter,
  room temperature and cubed
125 g (4½ oz) icing sugar, sifted
1 teaspoon of cake batter flavouring

To make the macaron shells:

Measure all ingredients before starting. Place a piping bag fitted with a round 2A piping tip in a milkshake cup or tall glass to support it when filling the bag. Place macaron-stencilled silicon mats on baking trays.

Sift icing sugar and almond meal into a bowl, discarding any chunks that don't easily pass through the sieve. Add 36 g (1¼ oz) egg whites to create an almond paste. Mix until combined, being careful not to over mix. Set aside.

Place the remaining 36 g (1¼ oz) egg whites in the bowl of a stand mixer with the whisk attachment.

Meanwhile, place the caster sugar and water in a saucepan with your sugar thermometer. Heat the sugar to 112°C (234°F). Once temperature is reached, turn the mixer on to low and whisk the egg whites, before gradually turning up the speed to the highest setting. Once the sugar syrup reaches 118°C (244°F), remove from the heat and turn the mixer down to a low-medium setting. Slowly and carefully pour the sugar mixture into the egg whites, aiming to pour between the side of the bowl and the whisk attachment. Once all the sugar is poured in, turn the mixer back to the highest setting to make an Italian meringue.

Whisk until the bowl is cool to the touch.

Fold one-third of the meringue into the almond paste at a time, until the mixture forms a ribbon. Transfer the mixture into your prepared piping bag and pipe 50 macaron shells onto the mats.

Tap the baking trays gently on the bench to knock out any air bubbles. Sprinkle rainbow nonpareils over the macaron shells.

Leave the macarons to sit at room temperature for at least 30 minutes, to form a skin. At this time, preheat the oven to 160°C (350°F) and when ready, bake the macarons for 12 minutes, opening the door very briefly halfway through to release excess steam.

Once the macarons have baked, allow them to cool completely before flipping half of them over so the flat surface is facing upwards. In the meantime, prepare the buttercream filling.

STORAGE
Assembled macarons will keep for up to 7 days refrigerated, just be sure to leave them at room temperature for 30 minutes before eating as they are best enjoyed at room temperature. Assembled macarons can be frozen on the same day you bake them, for up to 1 month. To thaw, place the macarons in the fridge for at least 1 hour with plastic wrap over the container to capture any condensation.

To make the buttercream filling:

Place the butter in the bowl of a stand mixer with the paddle attachment and beat on high speed for 5–10 minutes, scraping down the sides of the bowl as required.

Once the butter is glossy and pale in colour, turn the speed to low and add the sifted icing sugar. Beat for a further 5–10 minutes.

Finally, add the cake batter flavouring and beat until combined.

To assemble, pipe the buttercream filling onto the flat base of half of the macaron shells, then lightly push an uniced shell on top to sandwich the shells together.

Choc Raspberry Macarons

My favourite filling inside a macaron is chocolate ganache. A ganache takes a little more effort than a buttercream, but your patience will be rewarded when you taste the silky smooth centre (just be sure to use high-quality chocolate). The addition of tart raspberry to this dark chocolate ganache makes this flavour a crowd-pleaser.

MAKES: 50 SHELLS (25 MACARONS)
PREPARATION TIME: 20 MINUTES
COOKING TIME: 12 MINUTES
COOLING TIME: 20 MINUTES

For the chocolate ganache filling:
120 g (4¼ oz) dark chocolate, roughly chopped
20 g (¾ oz) unsalted butter
120 ml (4¼ fl oz) thickened cream
1 teaspoon of raspberry flavouring

For the macaron shells:
ALMOND PASTE:
100 g (3½ oz) icing sugar, sifted
100 g (3½ oz) almond meal, sifted
36 g (1¼ oz) egg whites, room temperature
1 teaspoon of dark pink food colouring gel
MERINGUE:
36 g (1¼ oz) egg whites, room temperature
100 g (3½ oz) caster sugar
25 ml (2 teaspoons) water

To make the chocolate ganache filling:

The chocolate ganache requires about 2 hours to set, so I recommend making this first. You can make the ganache up to a week in advance and store it in the fridge – just be sure to allow it to come to room temperature before using.

Place chocolate and butter in a heatproof bowl and set aside.

Place cream in a microwave-safe bowl and microwave for 15-second intervals until it just begins to bubble (about 45 seconds). Alternatively, you can heat the cream over medium-high heat in a saucepan until it starts to boil.

Pour the cream over the chocolate and butter. Leave to sit for a few minutes. Add the raspberry flavouring and gently stir.

Use a stick blender (or a spoon if you don't have one) to mix the ganache until the mixture becomes smooth and glossy.

Press a piece of plastic wrap on top of the ganache to prevent a skin from forming. Place in the fridge to chill for about 2 hours.

To make the macaron shells:

Measure all ingredients before starting. Place a piping bag fitted with a round 2A piping tip in a milkshake cup or tall glass to support it when filling the bag. Place macaron-stencilled silicon mats on baking trays.

Sift icing sugar and almond meal in a bowl, discarding chunks that don't easily pass through the sieve. Add 36 g (1¼ oz) egg whites to create an almond paste. Mix until combined, being careful not to over mix. Finally, add the food colouring gel and mix until just combined. Set aside.

Place the remaining 36 g (1¼ oz) egg whites in the bowl of a stand mixer with the whisk attachment.

Meanwhile, place the caster sugar and water in a saucepan with your sugar thermometer. Heat the sugar to 112°C (234°F). Once temperature is reached, turn the mixer on to low and whisk the egg whites, before

gradually turning up the speed to the highest setting. Once the sugar syrup reaches 118°C (244°F), remove from the heat and turn the mixer down to a low-medium setting. Slowly and carefully pour the sugar mixture into the egg whites, aiming to pour between the side of the bowl and the whisk attachment. Once all the sugar is poured in, turn the mixer back to the highest setting to make an Italian meringue.

Whisk until the bowl is cool to the touch.

Fold one-third of the meringue into the almond paste at a time, until the mixture forms a ribbon. Transfer the mixture into your prepared piping bag and pipe 50 macaron shells onto the mats.

Tap the baking trays gently on the bench to knock out any air bubbles.

Leave the macarons to sit at room temperature for at least 30 minutes, to form a skin. At this time, preheat the oven to 160°C (350°F) and when ready, bake the macarons for 12 minutes, opening the door very briefly halfway through to release excess steam.

Once the macarons have baked, allow them to cool completely before flipping half of them over so the flat surface is facing upwards.

To assemble, pipe the ganache filling onto the flat base of half the macaron shells, then lightly push an uniced shell on top to sandwich the shells together.

STORAGE
Assembled macarons will keep for up to 7 days refrigerated, just be sure to leave them at room temperature for 30 minutes before eating as they are best enjoyed at room temperature. Assembled macarons can be frozen on the same day you bake them, for up to 1 month. To thaw, place the macarons in the fridge for at least 1 hour with plastic wrap over the container to capture any condensation.

Lemon Meringue Macarons

Creamy and tangy, these Lemon Meringue Macarons are packed with flavour once you reach the centre and bite into a generous serving of homemade lemon curd. Popular throughout the year, they become even bigger sellers during the warmer months, when visitors swap the rich chocolate fillings for lighter, tangy options like these.

MAKES: 50 SHELLS (25 MACARONS)
PREPARATION TIME: 20 MINUTES
COOKING TIME: 12 MINUTES
COOLING TIME: 20 MINUTES

For the macaron shells:
ALMOND PASTE:
100 g (3½ oz) icing sugar, sifted
100 g (3½ oz) almond meal, sifted
36 g (1¼ oz) egg whites, room temperature
1 teaspoon of dark yellow food colouring gel
MERINGUE:
36 g (1¼ oz) egg whites, room temperature
100 g (3½ oz) caster sugar
25 ml (2 teaspoons) water

For the buttercream filling:
125 g (4½ oz) unsalted butter, room temperature and cubed
125 g (4½ oz) icing sugar, sifted
1 teaspoon of vanilla essence

1 batch of Lemon Curd (see page 290)

STORAGE
Assembled macarons will keep for up to 7 days refrigerated, just be sure to leave them at room temperature for 30 minutes before eating as they are best enjoyed at room temperature. Assembled macarons can be frozen on the same day you bake them, for up to 1 month. To thaw, place the macarons in the fridge for at least 1 hour with plastic wrap over the container to capture any condensation.

To make the macaron shells

Measure all ingredients before starting. Place a piping bag fitted with a round 2A piping tip in a milkshake cup or tall glass to support it when filling the bag. Place macaron-stencilled silicon mats on baking trays.

Sift icing sugar and almond meal into a bowl, discarding any chunks that don't easily pass through the sieve. Add 36 g (1¼ oz) egg whites to create an almond paste. Mix until combined, being careful not to over mix. Add the gel food colouring and mix until just combined. Set aside.

Place the remaining 36 g (1¼ oz) egg whites in the bowl of a stand mixer with the whisk attachment.

Meanwhile, place the caster sugar and water in a saucepan with your sugar thermometer. Heat the sugar to 112°C (234°F). Once temperature is reached, turn the mixer on to low and whisk the egg whites, before gradually turning up the speed to the highest setting. Once the sugar syrup reaches 118°C (244°F), remove from the heat and turn the mixer down to a low-medium setting. Slowly and carefully pour the sugar mixture into the egg whites, aiming to pour between the side of the bowl and the whisk attachment. Once all the sugar is poured in, turn the mixer back to the highest setting to make an Italian meringue.

Whisk until the bowl is cool to the touch.

Fold one-third of the meringue into the almond paste at a time until the mixture forms a ribbon. Transfer the mixture into your prepared piping bag and pipe 50 macaron shells onto the mats.

Tap the baking trays lightly on the bench to knock out any air bubbles.

Leave the macarons to sit at room temperature for at least 30 minutes, to form a skin. At this time, preheat the oven to 160°C (350°F) and when ready, bake the macarons for 12 minutes, opening the door very briefly halfway through to release excess steam.

→

Once the macarons have baked, allow them to cool completely before flipping half of them over so the flat surface is facing upwards. In the meantime, prepare the buttercream filling.

To make the buttercream filling:

Place the butter in the bowl of a stand mixer with the paddle attachment and beat for 5–10 minutes, scraping down the sides of the bowl as required.

Once the butter is glossy and pale in colour, turn the speed to low and add the icing sugar and vanilla. Beat for a further 5–10 minutes.

To assemble, pipe the buttercream filling onto the flat base of half of the macaron shells in a circle, with a hole in the middle for the Lemon Curd. Next, pipe Lemon Curd in the centre and lightly push an uniced shell on top to sandwich the shells together

Lavender Honey Macarons

I never expected this flavour of macaron to be a bestseller at Brooki Bakehouse, but it totally surprised me as soon as it hit the shelves. If you fancy the fragrance of lavender, the best way to enjoy it, in my opinion, is with the added sweetness of honey that lingers on the tongue after each bite. The secret to using lavender in your baked goods is to taste as you go, ensuring you use just the right amount, without overpowering the macaron biscuit.

MAKES: 50 SHELLS (25 MACARONS)
PREPARATION TIME: 20 MINUTES
COOKING TIME: 12 MINUTES
COOLING TIME: 20 MINUTES

For the macaron shells:
ALMOND PASTE:
100 g (3½ oz) icing sugar, sifted
100 g (3½ oz) almond meal, sifted
36 g (1¼ oz) egg whites, room temperature
1 teaspoon of purple food colouring gel
MERINGUE:
36 g (1¼ oz) egg whites, room temperature
100 g (3½ oz) caster sugar
25 ml (2 teaspoons) water

For the lavender honey buttercream filling:
125 g (4½ oz) unsalted butter, room temperature and cubed
125 g (4½ oz) icing sugar, sifted
½ teaspoon of lavender flavouring
1 teaspoon of honey

STORAGE
Assembled macarons will keep for up to 7 days refrigerated, just be sure to leave them at room temperature for 30 minutes before eating as they are best enjoyed at room temperature. Assembled macarons can be frozen on the same day you bake them, for up to 1 month. To thaw, place the macarons in the fridge for at least 1 hour with plastic wrap over the container to capture any condensation.

Measure all ingredients before starting. Place a piping bag fitted with a round 2A piping tip in a milkshake cup or tall glass to support it when filling the bag. Place macaron-stencilled silicon mats on baking trays.

Sift icing sugar and almond meal into a bowl, discarding any chunks that don't easily pass through the sieve. Add 36 g (1¼ oz) egg whites to create an almond paste. Mix until combined, being careful not to over mix. Add the gel food colouring and mix until just combined. Set aside.

Place the remaining 36 g (1¼ oz) egg whites in the bowl of a stand mixer with the whisk attachment.

Meanwhile, place the caster sugar and water in a saucepan with your sugar thermometer. Heat the sugar to 112°C (234°F). Once temperature is reached, turn the mixer on to low and whisk the egg whites, before gradually turning up the speed to the highest setting. Once the sugar syrup reaches 118°C (244°F), remove from the heat and turn the mixer down to a low-medium setting. Slowly and carefully pour the sugar mixture into the egg whites, aiming to pour between the side of the bowl and the whisk attachment. Once all the sugar is poured in, turn the mixer back to the highest setting to make an Italian meringue.

Whisk until the bowl is cool to the touch.

Fold one-third of the meringue into the almond paste at a time unti the mixture forms a ribbon. Transfer the mixture into your prepared piping bag and pipe 50 macaron shells onto the mats.

Tap the macarons gently on the bench to knock out any air bubbles.

Leave the macarons to sit at room temperature for at least 30 minutes, to form a skin. At this time preheat the oven to 160°C (350°F) and when ready, bake the macarons for 12 minutes, opening the door very briefly halfway through to release excess steam.

Once the macarons have baked, allow them to cool completely before flipping half of them over so the flat surface is facing upwards.. In the meantime, prepare the lavender honey buttercream filling.

To make the lavender honey buttercream filling:

Place the butter in the bowl of a stand mixer with the paddle attachment and beat for 5–10 minutes, scraping down the sides of the bowl as required.

Once the butter is glossy and pale in colour, turn the speed to low and add the sifted icing sugar. Beat for a further 5–10 minutes until light and fluffy.

Add the flavouring and honey, and beat until combined.

To assemble, pipe the buttercream filling onto the flat base of half of the macaron shells, then lightly push an uniced shell on top to sandwich the shells together.

Salted Caramel Macarons

The bestselling type of macaron at the bakery is salted caramel, which I'm sure is a surprise to no-one. This flavour is highly addictive, especially with the homemade salted caramel ganache filling, which provides a rich caramel taste with just the right amount of salt. It's impossible to stop at just one!

MAKES: 50 SHELLS (25 MACARONS)
PREPARATION TIME: 20 MINUTES
COOKING TIME: 12 MINUTES
COOLING TIME: 20 MINUTES

For the salted caramel ganache filling:
1 batch of Salted Caramel Sauce (see page 300)
230 g (8 oz) white chocolate, broken into pieces

For the macaron shells:
ALMOND PASTE:
100 g (3½ oz) icing sugar, sifted
100 g (3½ oz) almond meal, sifted
36 g (1¼ oz) egg whites, room temperature
MERINGUE:
36 g (1¼ oz) egg whites, room temperature
100 g (3½ oz) caster sugar
25 ml (2 teaspoons) water

To make the salted caramel ganache filling:

First, make the Salted Caramel Sauce. Once cooled, transfer the sauce to the bowl of a stand mixer.

Place the white chocolate in a microwave-safe bowl and heat in 15-second intervals until just melted (be careful not to overheat it). Alternatively, you can melt the chocolate over medium-high heat in a bowl over a saucepan of gently simmering water.

Pour the white chocolate over the Salted Caramel Sauce and beat until combined with the paddle attachment. Transfer to a bowl and press a piece of plastic wrap on top of the ganache to prevent a skin from forming. Place in the fridge to chill for 1–2 hours.

To make the macaron shells:

Measure all ingredients before starting. Place a piping bag fitted with a round 2A piping tip in a milkshake cup or tall glass to support it when filling the bag. Place macaron-stencilled silicon mats on baking trays.

Sift icing sugar and almond meal into a bowl, discarding any chunks that don't easily pass through the sieve. Add 36 g (1¼ oz) egg whites to create an almond paste. Mix until combined, being careful not to over mix. Set aside.

Place the remaining 36 g (1¼ oz) egg whites in another stand mixer bowl with the whisk attachment.

Meanwhile, place the caster sugar and water in a saucepan with your sugar thermometer. Heat the sugar to 112°C (234°F). Once temperature is reached, turn the mixer on to low and whisk the egg whites, before gradually turning up the speed to the highest setting. Once the sugar syrup reaches 118°C (244°F), remove from the heat and turn the mixer down to a low-medium setting. Slowly and carefully pour the sugar mixture into the egg whites, aiming to pour between the side of the bowl and the whisk attachment. Once all the sugar is poured in, turn the mixer back to the highest setting to make an Italian meringue.

Whisk until the bowl is cool to the touch.

→

Fold one-third of the meringue into the almond paste at a time until the mixture forms a ribbon. Transfer the mixture into your prepared piping bag and pipe 50 macaron shells onto the mats.

Tap the baking trays gently on the bench to knock out any air bubbles.

Leave the macarons to sit at room temperature for at least 30 minutes, to form a skin. At this time, preheat the oven to 160°C (350°F) and when ready, bake the macarons for 12 minutes, opening the door very briefly halfway through to release excess steam.

Once the macarons have baked, allow them to cool completely before flipping half of them over so the flat surface is facing upwards.

To assemble, pipe the salted caramel ganache filling onto the flat base of half of the macaron shells, then lightly push an uniced shell on top to sandwich the shells together.

STORAGE
Assembled macarons will keep for up to 7 days refrigerated, just be sure to leave them at room temperature for 30 minutes before eating as they are best enjoyed at room temperature. Assembled macarons can be frozen on the same day you bake them, for up to 1 month. To thaw, place the macarons in the fridge for at least 1 hour with plastic wrap over the container to capture any condensation.

Ferrero Rocher Macarons

When you unwrap the gold foil of a Ferrero Rocher, you know you are about to taste a deliciously rich, creamy hazelnut ganache, with the crispy crunch of hazelnut wafer to make for the perfect bite. That is exactly what I wanted to re-create with this macaron, which matches the Ferrero perfectly.

MAKES: 50 SHELLS (25 MACARONS)
PREPARATION TIME: 20 MINUTES
COOKING TIME: 12 MINUTES
COOLING TIME: 20 MINUTES

For the chocolate ganache filling:
160 ml (5½ fl oz) thickened cream
220 g (7¾ oz) Nutella
80 g (2¾ oz) milk chocolate, melted

For the macaron shells:
ALMOND PASTE:
100 g (3½ oz) icing sugar, sifted
100 g (3½ oz) almond meal, sifted
36 g (1¼ oz) egg whites, room temperature
1 teaspoon of brown food colouring gel
MERINGUE:
36 g (1¼ oz) egg whites, room temperature
100 g (3½ oz) caster sugar
25 ml (2 teaspoons) water

25 whole hazelnuts

STORAGE
Assembled macarons will keep for up to 7 days refrigerated, just be sure to leave them at room temperature for 30 minutes before eating as they are best enjoyed at room temperature. Assembled macarons can be frozen on the same day you bake them, for up to 1 month. To thaw, place the macarons in the fridge for at least 1 hour with plastic wrap over the container to capture any condensation.

To make the chocolate ganache filling:

The chocolate ganache requires at least 2 hours to set, so I recommend making this first. You can make the ganache up to a week in advance and store it in the fridge – just be sure to allow it to come to room temperature before using.

Place cream in a saucepan and heat over medium-high heat until it starts to boil. Remove from the heat.

Place the Nutella and chocolate into a bowl and pour over the hot cream. Leave to sit for a few minutes.

Use a stick blender (or a spoon if you don't have one) to mix the ganache until it becomes smooth and glossy.

Press a piece of plastic wrap on top of the ganache to prevent a skin from forming. Place in the fridge to chill for at least 2 hours (overnight is best). If making ganache in advance, remove from the fridge 1 hour before using and mix vigorously to return to a consistency that can easily be piped onto the macaron shells.

To make the macaron shells:

Measure all ingredients before starting. Place a piping bag fitted with a round 2A piping tip in a milkshake cup or tall glass to support it when filling the bag. Place macaron-stencilled silicon mats on baking trays.

Sift icing sugar and almond meal into a bowl and discard chunks that don't easily pass through the sieve. Add 36 g (1¼ oz) egg whites to create an almond paste. Mix until combined, being careful not to over mix. Add the gel food colouring and mix until just combined. Set aside.

Place the remaining 36 g (1¼ oz) egg whites in the bowl of a stand mixer with the whisk attachment.

Meanwhile, place the caster sugar and water in a saucepan with your sugar thermometer. Heat the sugar to 112°C (234°F). Once temperature is reached, turn the mixer on to low and whisk the egg whites, before gradually turning up the speed to the highest setting. Once the sugar syrup reaches 118°C (244°F), remove from the heat and turn the mixer down to a low-medium setting. Slowly and carefully pour the sugar mixture into the egg whites, aiming to pour between the side of the bowl and the whisk attachment. Once all the sugar is poured in, turn the mixer back to the highest setting to make an Italian meringue.

Whisk until the bowl is cool to the touch.

Fold one-third of the meringue into the almond paste at a time until the mixture forms a ribbon. Transfer the mixture into your prepared piping bag and pipe 50 macaron shells on to the mats.

Tap the baking trays gently on the bench to knock out any air bubbles.

Leave the macarons to sit at room temperature for at least 30 minutes, to form a skin. At this time, preheat the oven to 160°C (350°F) and when ready, bake the macarons for 12 minutes, opening the door very briefly halfway through to release excess steam.

Once the macarons have baked, allow them to cool completely before flipping half of them over so the flat surface is facing upwards.

To assemble, pipe the chocolate ganache filling onto the flat base of half of the macaron shells, place a whole hazelnut onto the filling in the centre, then lightly push an uniced shell on top to sandwich the shells together.

FAIL-SAFE MACARONS, ONE STEP AT A TIME

I love making macarons. I also think they get an unfair rap for being difficult to make when, in reality, they shouldn't be. Whenever you approach a new recipe for something you have not cooked before, it can be a little daunting. But the truth is, all you have to do is carefully read through the method one step at a time, envision yourself going through each step, and suddenly the recipe – like a symphony – starts to take shape. Macarons are no exception; you just have to take it one step at a time.

The easiest way to understand macarons is to break them down into parts. The first stage is to make the shells. The perfect shell will be crispy on the outside, soft and chewy at the centre. From there, each shell is matched up with its perfect pair and the filling is made. Fillings include buttercreams, pastry creams, jams and ganache. Each macaron flavour should have a distinguishable taste that is instantly recognisable once bitten into.

There are only four ingredients in a macaron shell. The science of a macaron has little to do with the ingredients and everything to do with the method of controlling the amount of air that is incorporated into the mixture. Folding the meringue into the almond paste, which is known as macaronage, is therefore the most important stage of making macarons. The importance of this step cannot be understated! You want the mixture to be fully incorporated and slowly run off the spatula in a ribbon-like consistency (after around 3–4 minutes of folding). Be careful not to over fold the batter, as otherwise the macarons won't hold their shape once piped onto the silicone mats. Master this and you've mastered the art of macarons.

So what are the secrets to perfect macarons? Well, this is one of those recipes where you've really got to pay attention to the details. Start by measuring your ingredients down to the exact gram. Sift the dry ingredients to ensure no crumbs form. And when adding colour, be sure to use gel colours for the best results. Checking the temperature of your oven prior to baking is also essential, so this is where an oven thermometer will come in handy. Open the door halfway through baking your macarons to release excess steam quickly, but as is always the case with baking, never open the oven until you are at least past the halfway point!

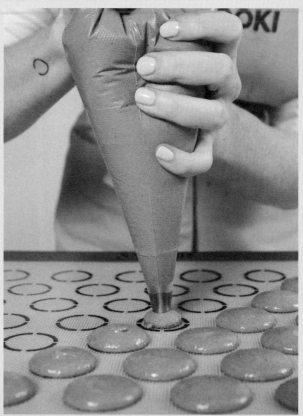

If your first batch of macarons didn't quite turn out as you hoped, then fear not. The good news is that many bakers make the same mistakes when it comes to macarons – myself included, when I first started making them. If you're wondering where you went wrong, consider this troubleshooting guide a cheat sheet to get it right next time and ensure you improve, one batch at a time.

PROBLEM:
Cracked tops.

SOLUTION:
1. The most common reason this occurs is that you haven't allowed the macaron shells to rest long enough to dry out before placing them in the oven. You will know the macarons are sufficiently rested when the surface looks matte (instead of glossy) and does not stick to your finger if you lightly tap one on top.

2. Cracked shells can also be the result of an underwhipped meringue that has not reached stiff peaks prior to the dry ingredients being folded in.

3. Another reason for cracked shells is that the oven temperature is too high or the baking trays are too close to the heat source. This is why an oven thermometer is a great investment to check the true temperature of your oven. For best results, ensure you always bake in the centre of the oven.

PROBLEM:
Lumpy shells.

SOLUTION:
This is most commonly caused by not sifting the almond meal and icing sugar together properly to remove any large clumps. Sifting the two ingredients together thoroughly will ensure an evenly distributed dry mixture and reduce the chance of any lumps sneaking through.

PROBLEM:
Air bubbles.

SOLUTION:
This one is an easy fix! To avoid air bubbles in your macarons, before baking, gently tap the baking trays a few times on the bench to knock the air out. Do this on a tea towel if you'd like to reduce the noise (or save your bench!).

PROBLEM:
Flat shells with no 'feet'.

SOLUTION:
1. When macarons bake in the oven, they should rise and create what is referred to as 'feet' at the base of the shell. Without them, the macaron shells are crispy and deflated, and may spread as they bake. This is commonly caused by overmixing the batter and incorporating too much air, when instead you should be folding the batter until it pours off a spatula like a ribbon – slow and steady.

2. Another reason macarons can flatten in the baking process is the use of too much colour, which adds more moisture and causes the macarons to deflate when baked.

PROBLEM:
Hollow shells.

SOLUTION:
The most common cause of hollow macaron shells is piping too high above the baking paper or silicone mat. Be sure to pipe close to the mat, slow and steady, to ensure evenly sized shells that have a uniform amount of macaron mixture throughout.

DESSERTS

Desserts and I go back a long way. Having lived more than half my life as a vegetarian, this is the one course of the meal where I am spoiled for choice, so I *always* save room for dessert. After all, one of my first ventures was opening a late-night dessert restaurant in my home town, featuring a menu of my favourite desserts from all over the world – classics like banoffee pie, sticky date pudding and apple crumble. But it was the brown butter skillet cookies that would become the talk of the town, selling out every night. And guess what? Every single one of these recipes appears here in this chapter, tried, tested and perfected over many years.

Sticky Date Puddings

If there's one dessert recipe I am particularly proud of, it is my Sticky Date Puddings. Ironically, I don't even like dates. But the use of bicarbonate of soda in this recipe, together with the assistance of a water bath to steam the cake as it cooks, creates a melt-in-mouth texture. This is the kind of recipe you save in your dinner party arsenal to wow your guests during the final act.

MAKES: 6 PUDDINGS
PREPARATION TIME: 15 MINUTES
COOKING TIME: 25–30 MINUTES

200 g (7 oz) dates, roughly chopped
180 ml (6 fl oz) water
1 teaspoon of bicarbonate of soda
70 g (2½ oz) butter, room temperature
180 g (6¼ oz) light brown sugar
2 large eggs, room temperature
140 g (5 oz) self-raising flour, sifted

1 batch of Butterscotch Sauce (see page 303)
  and vanilla ice-cream, to serve

Preheat the oven to 160°C (350°F). Grease six ramekins.

Place the dates and water in a saucepan and bring to the boil over medium heat. Once simmering, remove from the heat and sprinkle over the bicarbonate of soda, which will cause the mixture to bubble. Stir until completely mixed and then set aside to cool.

Meanwhile, in the bowl of a stand mixer with the paddle attachment, beat the butter and sugar on medium-high speed until pale in colour.

Add the eggs one at a time, beating until just combined.

Add the date mixture and self-raising flour, mixing until just combined.

Pour the batter into the greased ramekins, filling two-thirds of the way up.

Place the puddings in a deep roasting pan and pour in warm water until it reaches one-third of the way up the sides of the ramekins. Bake in the water bath for 25–30 minutes, or until a skewer comes out clean. Once baked, carefully remove the ramekins from the water bath and set aside to cool.

Once cooled, turn out the ramekins and gently tap to release.

To serve, pour hot Butterscotch Sauce over the puddings and scoop vanilla ice-cream on top to finish.

STORAGE
Store in an airtight container in the fridge for up to 1 week, or store in the freezer for up to 1 month.

Flourless Chocolate Cake (GF)

Flourless chocolate cake has a deserved reputation as one of the most beloved desserts on the planet, period. It is also a great option sans gluten, as it is naturally gluten-free but doubly delicious.

This incredibly simple cake will only take a few minutes to put together, making it a great last-minute recipe to keep up your sleeve for emergencies.

SERVES: 8–10
PREPARATION TIME: 10 MINUTES
COOKING TIME: 30 MINUTES
COOLING TIME: 2 HOURS

200 g (7 oz) dark chocolate, roughly chopped
175 g (6 oz) unsalted butter
70 g (2½ oz) light brown sugar
4 large eggs, room temperature
200 g (7 oz) almond meal

cocoa powder, to finish

Preheat the oven to 170°C (375°F). Grease and line a 20 cm (8") round cake tin with baking paper.

Melt the chocolate and butter in a saucepan over low heat until fully melted, stirring until combined. Set aside to cool.

In the bowl of a stand mixer with the paddle attachment, combine the cooled chocolate mixture with the sugar. Add the eggs one at a time, mixing between each addition. Mix in the almond meal until just combined.

Pour into the prepared tin and bake for 30 minutes or until a skewer comes out clean.

Allow to cool for 10 minutes before turning out onto a wire rack.

Once the cake is fully cooled, dust over some cocoa powder.

STORAGE
Store in an airtight container in a cool, dry place for up to 3 days.

Brown Butter Skillet Cookie

Whenever I have people over to my house for the first time, I make this dessert. It's a guaranteed showstopper every time and, better yet, it is the easiest thing to make. Having a quick and easy dessert to prepare beforehand is one of my best tips for a successful dinner party. As the evening draws to a close, you can easily whip out this skillet cookie and satisfy your guests utterly before they leave (take it from me – once you bite into this bad boy, it is impossible to stop!).

SERVES: 4
PREPARATION TIME: 15 MINUTES
COOKING TIME: 15–20 MINUTES
COOLING TIME: 10 MINUTES

170 g (6 oz) unsalted butter
100 g (3½ oz) caster sugar
165 g (5¾ oz) light brown sugar
1 egg + 1 egg yolk, room temperature
1 teaspoon of vanilla extract
pinch of salt
1 teaspoon of bicarbonate soda
270 g (9½ oz) plain flour
130 g (4½ oz) milk or dark chocolate chips

vanilla ice-cream and Hot Chocolate Fudge Sauce
  (see page 298), to serve

Preheat the oven to 180°C (400°F) and lightly grease a 20 cm (8") skillet pan.

To brown the butter, place in a saucepan and heat over medium until it melts, stirring continuously. Once melted, the butter will begin to foam around the edges; keep stirring. In about 5 minutes, the butter will turn golden brown. Some foam will subside and you'll see the butter has changed to a toasted brown colour. The butter is browned when it smells nutty. Remove from the stove.

Place the sugars into a bowl and, using a sieve, pour over the melted butter. Whisk to combine.

Add the egg and egg yolk, vanilla, salt, bicarbonate of soda and flour, mixing to combine. Set aside to cool.

Once cool, fold in the chocolate chips and transfer to the prepared pan.

Bake for 15–20 minutes or until golden on top. Remove the cookie from the oven carefully, as it will be extra hot. Allow to cool for 10 minutes before topping with ice-cream and Hot Chocolate Fudge Sauce.

STORAGE
This cookie is best enjoyed warm from the oven, though will store at room temperature in an airtight container for up to 3 days.

Apple Crumble

Growing up in Tasmania as I did, you learn to love winter – not by choice, but by design. There are quite a few months of winter to get through, with sub-zero temperatures and grey skies leaving you with only one choice: winter desserts. My favourite dessert as a kid was apple crumble. And to this day, when I go back home, this is the dessert my mum will have ready on the table after dinner, as if nothing has ever changed.

SERVES: 8
PREPARATION TIME: 15 MINUTES
COOKING TIME: 25–30 MINUTES

For the filling:
1 kg (2 lb 3 oz) Granny Smith apples
50 ml (2 fl oz) water
100 g (3½ oz) white sugar
½ teaspoon of ground cinnamon

For the topping:
50 g (1¾ oz) rolled oats
200 g (7 oz) self-raising flour
180 g (6¼ oz) light brown sugar
1 teaspoon of ground cinnamon
125 g (4½ oz) unsalted butter, room temperature

vanilla ice-cream, to serve

To make the filling:

Preheat the oven to 180°C (400°F).

Peel and core the apples and slice thinly before placing in a medium saucepan with the water, sugar and cinnamon. Heat over medium until the apples are soft. Push the apples with a wooden spoon to break them down into a mushy consistency.

Transfer apples to a 24 cm (9") ovenproof dish or, for individual servings, 10 medium ramekins.

To make the topping:

Place all ingredients in a large bowl and mix with your hands until clumps form. Sprinkle over the apples and spread out evenly.

Bake for 25–30 minutes until golden brown on top.

Allow the crumble to stand for 10 minutes before serving.

Serve warm with vanilla ice-cream on top.

STORAGE
This dessert is best enjoyed warm, fresh from the oven. Store leftovers covered in the fridge and reheat in the oven for 10–15 minutes.

Pavlova (GF)

Nothing screams Australian summer like a pavlova – especially one piled with berries and freshly whipped cream. This pavlova is light and fresh, with passionfruit syrup drizzled on top for a bit of zing.

SERVES: 8–12
PREPARATION TIME: 30 MINUTES
COOKING TIME: 1 HOUR
COOLING TIME: 1–2 HOURS

4 large egg whites, room temperature
220 g (7 oz) caster sugar
2 teaspoons of cornflour
1 teaspoon of vanilla extract
1 teaspoon of lemon juice
500 ml (17 fl oz) thickened cream
500 g (1 lb 1oz) fresh mixed berries
170 g (6 oz) can passionfruit pulp in syrup,
  strained and seeds discarded

icing sugar, to serve

Preheat the oven to 140°C (325°F).

Line a baking tray with baking paper and draw a 24 cm (9") circle in the centre (an easy way to do this is to trace around a cake tin).

Make sure the bowl of your stand mixer is completely grease-free, as this recipe will not work if there's any fat residue on the bowl or the whisk.

In the bowl of a stand mixer with the whisk attachment, beat egg whites on high speed until the egg whites start to foam and increase in size. Gradually add the sugar 1 tablespoon at a time, beating well after each addition. Continue until all the sugar has been added and incorporated.

Turn the mixer to low and beat in the cornflour, vanilla and lemon juice.

Spoon the mixture inside the circle on the baking paper and spread out towards the outside edge of the circle using a metal spoon. Create a slight well by building the walls a bit taller, leaving a depression in the centre for the fresh fruit and cream once baked.

Reduce the oven temperature to 130°C (300°F) and bake for 1 hour.

Turn the oven off and leave the meringue inside with the door slightly ajar for 1–2 hours, until cooled completely.

Meanwhile, in the bowl of a stand mixer with the whisk attachment, beat cream until thickened and just holding its shape. Store in the fridge until ready to use.

To serve, top the meringue with whipped cream, berries, passionfruit syrup and a dusting of icing sugar.

STORAGE
Once decorated, the pavlova is best enjoyed on the same day. The meringue can be stored, undecorated, in an airtight container out of direct sunlight for up to 2 days.

All Roads Lead to Roman Gelato

When I think of Italy, I think of food. That's not to say I'm not interested in the epic history of the Roman Empire or the Renaissance architecture of the fourteenth to sixteenth centuries, but it certainly reveals where my priorities lie! You see, I'm not opposed to planning a travel itinerary entirely based around food. And when it comes to my travels in the Bel Paese, I could write a book of food diary entries expressing my love for Italian desserts – and have a particular fondness for a classic tiramisu! La dolce vita, after all.

They say all roads lead to Rome, so it is little wonder my adventure towards the sweet life began in the eternal city itself. I was seventeen years young when I first stepped foot in Europe. A year prior I had cut a deal with my father to chaperone me to any destination in the world where I could save enough money for a plane ticket. He didn't think much of it when the words left his mouth, but a year later I had my bags packed and hotels booked. We split the costs down the middle and were on our way.

When we landed in Rome I made a beeline for G. Fassi, the oldest gelateria in Rome and indisputably the best. In front of me was a sea of colour and delectable creamy textures – from pistachio and stracciatella all the way through to bourbon vanilla and tiramisu. I didn't understand half of the flavour labels, nor did I speak a word of Italian outside of the conversational niceties. But this being Italy, a friendly smile, an eager gesture and an expressive *Sì* three times in succession was enough to cement my choices. Wandering around the narrow cobblestoned streets of Rome with three gelato scoops piled into a waffle cone became my daily routine.

Tiramisu

If ever I feel like a classic dessert to tie off an evening, I make these Tiramisu glass jars. It's a great choice for pasta night and has just the right amount of booze in the base to end a meal.

SERVES: 6
PREPARATION TIME: 15 MINUTES
CHILLING TIME: 2 HOURS

240 ml (8 fl oz) strong coffee
1 tablespoon of Kahlúa (optional)
480 ml (1 pint) thickened cream
100 g (3½ oz) caster sugar
450 g (1 lb) mascarpone, room temperature
14 savoiardi biscuits
2 tablespoons of cocoa powder

Start by stirring the Kahlúa (if using) into the coffee. Set aside.

Place six glasses on the kitchen bench.

In the bowl of a stand mixer with the whisk attachment, beat the cream and sugar until stiff peaks form (be careful not to over mix).

Add the mascarpone and beat until creamy.

Transfer to a piping bag and cut a hole in the end. Pipe a small amount in the base of each glass.

For the next layer, dip a biscuit in the coffee and place inside the glass on top of the blob of mascarpone (you may need to break it into a couple of pieces). Pipe another blob into the glass on top of the biscuit, add another coffee-dipped biscuit and top with mascarpone. Repeat with the other glasses.

Dust the top of each one with cocoa and place in the fridge to set.

STORAGE
Store glasses covered with plastic wrap in the fridge for up to 3 days.

Lemon Meringue Tarts

Nothing beats a classic lemon tart. With a buttery base, zingy citrus centre and the deliciousness of warm meringue, there really is nothing not to love.

I like to make these as small tarts for individual serves, the perfect dessert to serve each of your dinner party guests.

SERVES: 8
PREPARATION TIME: 1 HOUR 45 MINUTES
COOKING TIME: 45 MINUTES
COOLING TIME: 4 HOURS OR OVERNIGHT

For the tart shells:
170 g (6 oz) unsalted butter, room temperature
120 g (4¼ oz) icing sugar
½ teaspoon of salt
1 large egg, room temperature
1 teaspoon of vanilla extract
350 g (12¼ oz) plain flour

For the lemon filling:
3 large eggs, room temperature
3 large egg yolks (keep the whites for the meringue), room temperature
150 g (5¼ oz) caster sugar
juice of 2 lemons
100 g (3½ oz) unsalted butter, room temperature

For the meringue:
3 large egg whites, room temperature
125 g (4½ oz) caster sugar
1 teaspoon of vanilla extract
1 teaspoon of cornflour
1 teaspoon of malt vinegar

STORAGE
Lemon tarts without meringue can be stored for up to 3 days in an airtight container at room temperature.

BROOKI'S TIP
If you don't have pie weights or baking beans, you can use uncooked rice instead to stop the pastry from rising when you bake the tart shells blind.

To make the tart shells:

In the bowl of a stand mixer with the paddle attachment, beat the butter on medium-high speed until creamy. Lower the speed to low and add the icing sugar and salt, mixing until just combined.

Mix in the egg and vanilla until completely combined. Add the flour and mix on low until just combined into a dough.

Remove from the bowl, cover with plastic wrap and press into a flattened disc. Chill in the fridge for at least 1 hour.

Once the dough has chilled, remove from the fridge and allow to sit at room temperature for 10 minutes.

Preheat the oven to 180°C (400°F) and grease eight 12 cm (4½") tart tins with cooking spray.

Roll the dough on a floured surface to a thickness of about 3 mm (⅛"), and use a knife to cut circles about 2.5 cm (1") wider than the tart tins. Press the dough into the tins, including the ridges, and trim the excess.

Use a fork to prick some holes in the bottom of the tart shells.

Place a small piece of aluminium foil into each tart shell and fill with pie weights or baking beans.

Bake for 15 minutes, then remove the pie weights and bake for a further 10 minutes, until golden brown. Allow the tart shells to cool completely before removing from the tins.

To make the lemon filling:

In a saucepan over medium heat, stir together the eggs, egg yolks, sugar and lemon juice. Continue stirring until the mixture thickens enough to coat the back of a spoon, about 15 minutes.

Stir in the butter and continue stirring until fully incorporated.

Remove from the heat, transfer to a bowl and place a piece of plastic wrap over the top, pressing down to prevent a skin from forming. Place in the fridge to cool completely.

Spoon filling into each tart shell until full. Chill in the fridge for at least 4 hours, or overnight.

To make the meringue:

In the bowl of a stand mixer with the whisk attachment, beat the egg whites on high speed until fluffy. Slowly add the sugar, 1 tablespoon at a time, until fully incorporated. Once stiff peaks have formed, add the vanilla, cornflour and vinegar, mixing until combined.

Transfer the meringue into a piping bag with your preferred piping tip and pipe the meringue on top of the tarts. Use a kitchen torch to toast the meringue before serving.

Chocolate Lava Cake

Chocolate lava cake (or molten cake) was the first dessert I ever learned to make. I was shocked by how easy it is to prepare and subsequently went through a period during which I would show off my newfound baking skills to anyone who would care to indulge. It's a classic in my rotation of desserts and I hope it will now be in yours, too.

SERVES: 4
PREPARATION TIME: 10 MINUTES
COOKING TIME: 12 MINUTES

170 g (6 oz) high-quality dark chocolate
110 g (3¾ oz) unsalted butter, room temperature
2 eggs + 2 egg yolks, room temperature
50 g (1¾ oz) caster sugar
pinch of salt
20 g (¾ oz) plain flour

vanilla ice-cream, to serve

Preheat the oven to 200°C (425°F). Generously spray four ramekins with cooking spray and set aside.

Pour a few centimetres of water in a saucepan and place over medium heat. Bring to a simmer. Place the chocolate and butter in a heatproof bowl and sit over the water to melt together. Once melted, whisk until the mixture is smooth.

In the bowl of a stand mixer with the paddle attachment, beat the eggs, egg yolks, sugar and salt until thickened and pale.

Fold the chocolate mix into the egg mixture, then fold in the flour.

Evenly distribute the batter between the ramekins and bake for 12 minutes, or until the cake is firm on the outside, but the centre is soft. It's important to keep your eye on this dessert to prevent it from overbaking! You want to ensure the molten cake is baked on the outside but soft and gooey in the centre (it should pour out like lava when you dip your spoon in).

Remove from the oven and allow the ramekins to sit for a few minutes before turning them out upside down onto a plate. Tap gently to ensure the bottom is not stuck. Serve immediately with a generous amount of vanilla ice-cream.

STORAGE
This dessert is best enjoyed immediately; however, you can store unbaked lava cakes in their ramekins in the fridge for up to 3 days if you prefer to make them in advance. If baking from refrigerated, allow an extra 1–2 minutes in the oven.

Banoffee Pie

With a buttery biscuit base, toffee filling, whipped cream and freshly sliced bananas on top, a banoffee pie really leaves little to the imagination. It is perfect the way it is. This classic Banoffee Pie is a favourite in our household and forever will be, though I should warn you, it is definitely on the sweeter side!

SERVES: 6
PREPARATION TIME: 30 MINUTES
COOLING TIME: 1 HOUR

For the base:
250 g (9 oz) digestive biscuits
125 g (4½ oz) butter, melted

For the caramel filling:
395 g (14 oz) can sweetened condensed milk
70 g (2½ oz) light brown sugar
50 g (1¾ oz) unsalted butter

For the topping:
300 ml (10 fl oz) thickened cream
2 ripe bananas, thinly sliced

Lightly grease six small tart tins.

To make the base:

Blitz the biscuits in a food processor to a fine crumb.

Transfer to a bowl, pour over melted butter and use your hands to combine. Divide the biscuit mix between six tart tins. Firmly press down with the back of a metal spoon to ensure the tart base is even on the bottom and up the sides. Place in the fridge to set.

To make the caramel filling:

Place condensed milk, sugar and butter in a medium saucepan over low heat. Stir continuously with a wooden spoon for 10–12 minutes or until the caramel thickens enough to coat the back of it. Set aside to cool before filling the tarts.

Pour the caramel into the tart tins and allow to chill in the fridge for at least 1 hour. Meanwhile, make the topping.

To make the topping:

In the bowl of a stand mixer with the whisk attachment, beat the cream until thickened and just holding its shape.

To assemble:

Place a dollop of cream onto each filled tart base and top with thin slices of banana.

STORAGE
This dessert is best enjoyed on the day it is made. However, you can store the tarts in an airtight container in the fridge for up to 1 week, before they have been topped with cream and banana.

Inspired in Istanbul

When I visited Istanbul, I discovered baklava for the first time. I was barely out of my teens and early in my worldly adventures, so I had little to no expectations prior to my arrival. I had no idea of how mesmerising the Bosphorus would be, nor that it was the geographical separation between Europe and Asia. And that's the humbling truth about travel – that you are forever a student, learning firsthand the history and cultures of the land on which you are standing.

If you haven't yet had the joy of discovering Middle Eastern desserts, consider baklava the opening act. This delicate treat is made of layers of crunchy filo pastry and chopped walnuts, all drowning in honey syrup. What more could you want from an afternoon treat?

It wasn't until a few years later that I would rediscover baklava, this time while island-hopping in Greece. I was on another one of my solo missions of self-discovery, which in my case also translated as food discovery, because it was a sensory discovery I could enjoy by myself. I was walking the streets of Mykonos in the early hours of the evening, filling the time between lunch and dinner with a quest to find something sweet. That was hardly a difficult task in Greece, where sweets reign supreme and are in abundance at every turn.

A few years later, I found myself discovering parts of the Middle East. On this third encounter with baklava, I realised that instead of stuffing both myself and my suitcase full of pastries on every trip, I should really learn how to make them myself. And when I returned to Australia, I did just that.

I had convinced myself that baklava would be difficult to make; in reality, it is one of the easiest desserts. Perhaps that was a lesson in itself: that just because something is foreign to you, it doesn't mean you can't master it. So much joy can come from learning recipes and techniques outside of your usual repertoire. Baking is as close as I have come to travelling and experiencing the world without ever leaving home. Let this be a reminder to try new things and use baking as a way to discover new flavours, textures and cultures. There's a whole world out there, right inside your kitchen.

Baklava

One of my fondest travel memories was the day I first discovered baklava in the windy, cobblestoned streets of Istanbul. I will never forget the sound of the crunch as I bit into the wafer-thin pastry layers, syrup running down my forearm as I tried to avoid wasting even a flake. I was delighted to find out, upon my return home, that baklava is not particularly difficult to make, and so my quest to re-create the perfect baklava began. That was more than 7 years ago and, to this day, I still use the same recipe.

MAKES: 30 PIECES
PREPARATION TIME: 45 MINUTES
COOKING TIME: 1 HOUR, 10 MINUTES
CHILLING TIME: OVERNIGHT

40 sheets of filo pastry
500 g (1 lb 1oz) walnuts
1 teaspoon of ground cinnamon
285 g (10 oz) unsalted butter, melted

For the syrup:
200 g (7 oz) caster sugar
2 tablespoons of lemon juice
185 ml (6 fl oz) water
170 g (6 oz) pure honey

If using frozen filo pastry, thaw at room temperature for 30 minutes before commencing.

Cut filo pastry to the same size as the base of a 33 × 23 cm (13 × 9") baking tin. Keep the pastry covered with a damp tea towel while you work.

Place the walnuts and cinnamon in a food processor and pulse to a fine crumb (but not a powder).

Preheat the oven to 160°C (350°F).

To build the baklava, start by brushing the tin with melted butter and layer one sheet of filo on top. Brush this layer with butter, top with filo, and continue until you have used 10 sheets of filo pastry. Scatter a fifth of the walnuts on top.

Continue to stack five more sheets of filo, brushing butter in between each later. Top with another fifth of the walnuts. Repeat this process three more times.

For the top layer, alternate the final 10 sheets of filo with a brush of butter in between each one.

Cut the baklava into four long strips, then cut diagonally to make diamond shapes.

Bake in the oven for 1 hour, or until golden brown. Meanwhile, make the syrup.

For the syrup:

Place all the syrup ingredients in a saucepan over medium-high heat. Bring to a simmer and continually stir, until the sugar dissolves. Reduce the heat to medium and simmer for another 3 minutes, before removing from the heat to cool.

When the baklava has baked, remove from the oven and immediately pour over the syrup. Leave to soak overnight at room temperature in an airtight container.

STORAGE
Store for up to 1 week at room temperature in an airtight container, out of direct sunlight.

BROOKI'S TIP
This recipe needs to sit for 6+ hours for the flavours to fully develop, so is best prepared a day in advance.

GIFTS FOR FRIENDS

As a baker, my friends never expect me to arrive empty-handed. And it just so happens that I have nailed a few core recipes that are quick to make and easy to clean up afterwards, but go a long way in sweetening my friendships! This chapter includes some incredibly easy bakes that will take no time at all and, what's more, you probably have most of the ingredients in your pantry already.

Chocolate Rum Balls

There's nothing groundbreaking about a rum ball, but I would be doing my childhood a disservice if I didn't include this recipe, because it is the one treat in the whole book I have consumed more of than anything else. I made these with my mum growing up, no matter the time of year – though they do make a particularly good Christmas present.

MAKES: APPROX. 24 BALLS
PREPARATION TIME: 10 MINUTES
COOLING TIME: 2 HOURS

250 g (9 oz) arrowroot biscuits
4 tablespoons of unsweetened cocoa powder
395 g (14 oz) can condensed milk
1 teaspoon of rum essence
85 g (3 oz) unsweetened desiccated coconut, to roll

Blitz the biscuits in a food processor to a fine crumb. Transfer to a large bowl and add the cocoa powder. Stir to combine.

Pour in the condensed milk and rum essence, and use your hands to mix together thoroughly. Allow the mixture to stand for 10 minutes before rolling.

Spread the coconut onto a large plate.

Roll the mixture into balls (slightly smaller than golf balls) and then roll in coconut.

Place in the fridge to set in an airtight container for at least 2 hours.

STORAGE
Store in the fridge in an airtight container for up to 1 week.

Salted Caramel Toffees

Another perfect stocking filler at Christmastime is these Salted Caramel Toffees. Working with sugar can be a little intimidating at first, but I promise that if you take one step at a time (be sure to read the recipe all the way through first), it is surprisingly easy.

MAKES: 56
COOKING TIME: 15 MINUTES
CHILLING TIME: OVERNIGHT

300 ml (10 fl oz) thickened cream
100 g (3½ oz) salted butter
330 g (11½ oz) sugar
250 g (9 oz) golden syrup
2 teaspoons of vanilla extract
1 teaspoon of sea salt flakes

Grease and line a 22 cm (8") square tin with baking paper, with a slight overhang over each side and set aside.

Place all ingredients except the salt in a large saucepan and heat on high, stirring occasionally until the sugar dissolves and the mixture comes to a boil, about 4–5 minutes.

Reduce heat to medium and place a sugar thermometer in the caramel mixture. Cook without stirring until the temperature reaches 121°C (250°F), around 9–12 minutes.

Remove from the heat and remove the thermometer. Allow the caramel to cool for a few minutes, before carefully pouring it into the prepared tin.

Sprinkle over sea salt flakes and set aside to cool overnight.

The next day, lift the caramel out of the tin using the overhanging baking paper and place on a cutting board. Cut the caramel into rectangles or squares with a long knife.

Use baking paper to wrap around the toffees and twist the ends to form a classic toffee wrapper.

STORAGE
Store at room temperature in an airtight container for up to 1 week.

The Tart Worth Travelling For

If there's one pastry I crave almost on the daily, it's a Portuguese tart. In fact, I'd go so far as to say that if I lived in Portugal, I'd start each day off with a tart, a cup of black coffee and a view of the ocean. Bliss.

I had barely landed in Portugal when I made a beeline for the world-famous Pastéis de Belém, an airy bakery located in the west of Lisbon. This bakery has a well-deserved reputation for being home to the world's best Portuguese tart, a bold claim I firmly believe to be true.

When you arrive at the bakery, there will almost always be a line. The kitchen is rumoured to make around 20,000 of these bite-sized treats every single day. But with many pastry shops around Lisbon and, indeed, all of Portugal, what makes this tart the best?

The secret to the perfect Portuguese tart is in the puff pastry, which should be light, crunchy and flaky. Because Pastéis de Belém churns out so many pastries, you're almost guaranteed your tart will be fresh out of the oven and still warm. This ensures a flaky exterior that is impossible to replicate – unless, of course, you master the art of making them at home!

Another secret to a mouth-watering Portuguese tart is the creamy custard filling. To ensure the filling melts in your mouth, it is important to avoid the addition of too much flour or starch. Keeping your filling custard-like and creamy will perfectly balance the flaky tart shell, topped off with a generous sprinkle of cinnamon and icing sugar.

IN TARTS
WE TRUST.

Portuguese Tarts

Portuguese tarts (pastéis de nata) hold a special place in my heart, as I discovered them when I was on my first solo trip to Europe at twenty years young. I wasn't very well travelled at the time, just wide-eyed and enthusiastic. I made the almost mandatory pilgrimage to Belém to visit the famous Pastéis de Belém bakery to see what all the fuss was about.

It was nothing short of a life-changing moment – I decided I wanted to learn to bake everything I discovered on my travels, and eventually became a bakery owner. This is my easy solution to making Portuguese tarts at home (full disclosure: the store-bought puff pastry is a handy cheat).

MAKES: 12
PREPARATION TIME: 25 MINUTES
COOKING TIME: 20 MINUTES
COOLING TIME: 45 MINUTES

1 large egg + 2 egg yolks, room temperature
115 g (4 oz) caster sugar
2 tablespoons of cornflour
200 ml (6½ fl oz) thickened cream
200 ml (6½ fl oz) full cream milk
2 teaspoons of vanilla extract
1 sheet of puff pastry

ground cinnamon and icing sugar, to finish

Whisk together the egg and yolks, sugar and cornflour in a saucepan until combined. Gradually whisk in the cream and milk until smooth.

Place the pan over a medium heat and cook, stirring continuously until the mixture thickens and comes to the boil.

Remove the saucepan from the heat and stir in the vanilla. Transfer the custard into a bowl and cover the surface with plastic wrap to prevent a skin from forming as it cools.

Preheat the oven to 200°C (425°F) and lightly grease a 12-hole muffin tray.

Cut the puff pastry sheet in half and put one half on top of the other, then set aside for 5 minutes.

Roll up the pastry tightly into a log, then cut it into 12 1-cm (½") rounds. Lay each pastry round on a lightly floured surface and use a rolling pin to roll out the pastry until each disc is very thin and 10 cm (4") in diameter.

Place the pastry discs into the muffin tray to make pastry cases, then spoon in the cooled custard to three-quarters full.

Bake for 20 minutes, or until the pastry and custard are golden and even slightly blackened in places.

Remove from the oven and leave the tarts in the tray for 5 minutes, then transfer to a wire rack to cool completely.

Dust with cinnamon and icing sugar to serve. I like to enjoy these still warm from the oven, but be careful not to indulge too soon, as they're piping hot when you first remove them!

STORAGE
Store in an airtight container at room temperature for up to 2 days. Reheat the tarts in the oven at 180°C (400°F) for a few minutes before serving, to puff them back to life.

Salted Caramel Meringues

This is another foolproof recipe provided by my mum, with my only adaptation being to swirl a big dollop of salted caramel through each meringue.

You could, of course, go without the caramel, or substitute with another addition like Nutella or freeze-dried raspberries.

SERVES: 4
PREPARATION TIME: 10 MINUTES
COOKING TIME: 2 HOURS
COOLING TIME: 2 HOURS

3 large egg whites, room temperature
170 g (6 oz) caster sugar
1 teaspoon of cornflour
½ teaspoon of malt vinegar
½ teaspoon of vanilla
1 batch of Salted Caramel Sauce (see page 300)

Make sure the bowl of your stand mixer is completely grease free, as this recipe will not work if there's any fat residue on the bowl or the whisk.

Preheat the oven to 160°C (350°F). Line two baking trays with baking paper.

In the bowl of a stand mixer with the whisk attachment, whisk egg whites until soft peaks form. Gradually add sugar, a tablespoon at a time, whisking well between each addition.

Once all the sugar has been added, continue to whisk on high for a few more minutes. Add the cornflour, vinegar and vanilla, and whisk to combine.

Scoop meringue into four piles onto lined trays. Spoon 1 tablespoon of Salted Caramel Sauce over each meringue and use a butter knife to swirl on top. Reduce the oven temperature to 140°C (325°F) and bake meringues for 30 minutes.

Reduce the temperature to 130°C (300°F) and bake for a further 30 minutes. Finally, reduce the temperature to 110°C (260°F) for the final 1 hour of baking.

Turn the oven off and allow the meringues to cool completely in the oven with the door slightly ajar.

STORAGE
Store in an airtight container at room temperature and out of direct sunlight for up to 1 week.

White Chocolate Rocky Road

Rocky Road is my go-to when I need to throw together a little something at the final hour to give to a friend. There are no real rules as to what you can mix in to your rocky road, but I do find the white chocolate version is the perfect treat at Christmastime.

MAKES: 12 PIECES
PREPARATION TIME: 5 MINUTES
COOKING TIME: 5 MINUTES
COOLING TIME: 2 HOURS

250 g (9 oz) marshmallows, chopped
100 g (3½ oz) Turkish delight, chopped
110 g (3¾ oz) macadamias, chopped
60 g (2 oz) pistachios
35 g (1¼ oz) unsweetened desiccated coconut
360 g (12¾ oz) white chocolate, chopped

Lightly grease a 20 cm (8") square cake tin and line with baking paper, allowing overhang on all sides.

Place the marshmallows, Turkish delight, nuts and coconut in a bowl.

Place chocolate in a microwave-safe bowl and heat until melted in 30 second intervals, stirring with a metal spoon each time, until just melted. Alternatively, you can melt the chocolate over medium-high heat in a bowl placed over a saucepan of gently simmering water until liquid. Be careful not to overheat the chocolate.

Pour chocolate over marshmallow mixture and mix well. Press into the prepared tin and refrigerate for 2 hours or until set.

To serve, remove from tin and cut into squares.

STORAGE
Store in an airtight container at room temperature and out of direct sunlight for up to 2 weeks.

Caramel Fudge

This Caramel Fudge is alarmingly easy to make and highly addictive, which probably explains why I would make myself a tray of it once a week during my university days, procrastibaking. These days I'm more likely to whip up a batch to gift to a sweet-toothed friend.

MAKES: 12 PIECES
PREPARATION TIME: 10 MINUTES
CHILLING TIME: 2 HOURS

125 g (4½ oz) butter
395 g (14 oz) can sweetened condensed milk
2 tablespoons of golden syrup
215 g (7½ oz) light brown sugar
120 g (4¼ oz) white chocolate, broken into pieces
  (or chips)

Line a 25 cm × 7 cm (10 × 3") baking tin with baking paper, allowing overhang on all sides.

Melt butter in a medium saucepan over low heat. Add condensed milk, golden syrup and brown sugar, and stir over low heat until boiling. Simmer for 10 minutes, stirring continuously.

Remove from heat and add white chocolate, stirring continuously until all the chocolate has melted and is fully incorporated.

Pour into the prepared tin, pushing the fudge into the corners to make sure the tray is evenly covered.

Allow to cool and refrigerate until firm (at least 2 hours). Cut into bite-sized pieces.

STORAGE
Fudge is best stored at room temperature and will keep for up to 2 weeks in an airtight container out of direct sunlight.

French Hot Chocolate

The first time I tasted this deliciously rich *chocolat chaud* was at Angelina tea house in Paris. At the time, I was twenty years old, travelling independently and had never experienced a love quite like it. The moment was completely transformative and I can say on good authority that if you've ever had the privilege of visiting Angelina, this hot chocolate recipe will take you right back there to the Rue de Rivoli.

SERVES: 4
COOKING TIME: 10 MINUTES

200 g (7 oz) 70% dark chocolate, roughly chopped
300 ml (10 fl oz) thickened cream
500 ml (17 fl oz) full cream milk

Place the chocolate and cream in a medium saucepan and stir constantly on low heat until a glossy ganache forms.

Add the milk and stir until the mixture combines completely. Bring back to a gentle simmer then pour into mugs to serve, or allow to cool and pour into milk bottles to gift to friends, to be reheated at a later date.

STORAGE
Store in an airtight container for up to 5 days in the fridge. Reheat in the microwave or over the stove for a freshly brewed cup!

One Day in Paris

My fascination with the City of Light started well before I arrived in Paris for the first time. I have long been enamoured with the history, culture and traditions of France. And there is perhaps no-one who celebrates culture and traditions as emphatically as the French, especially when it comes to longstanding patisseries and pastries!

Paris is home to some of the world's finest patisseries. That's not to say there aren't great pastries to be found outside of Paris (there certainly are). But with many of the world's most celebrated pastry chefs plying their trade within the city limits, it's hard for anywhere else to compete.

As I meandered along the streets of Paris on my first solo expedition, I found solace in the tea houses, boulangeries and, indeed, the fine French patisseries the city has to offer. My first experience of what I would now call 'real hot chocolate' was upon being seated at the famous Angelina tea house on Rue de Rivoli. I had heard whispers of the famous *chocolat chaud*, in all of its thick and decadent glory. While scrolling through the reviews on Tripadvisor, I'd noticed a recurring commentary about the hot chocolate being too rich or too thick, which struck me as a reason to try it.

I had never believed you could have too much chocolate. My parents both have a sweet tooth, so I inevitably grew up with one too. But until this moment, I had only ever experienced chocolate in the form of Cadbury milk chocolate. Dark chocolate was an anomaly to me and not particularly enticing. That was, until Paris.

Sitting inside the elegant tea house adorned with Belle Époque gold panelling and a Vincent Lorant-Heilbronn mural, I was transported to another time. A time when Coco Chanel would sit in the same room. As I sat at a marble table, surrounded by people wearing puffer jackets and beanies, I imagined myself being here in a previous life. And so began my penchant for transporting myself to other times and places with food, which in turn led me to re-create all of my favourite pastries from around the world back home in Australia, where I could introduce customers to them, many for the first time.

When my *chocolat chaud* arrived a daydream later, I brought the jug up to my face and inhaled. Rich, dark chocolate that you could almost taste, simply by smelling it. Slowly and carefully I poured a cupful almost to the brim, allowing just enough room for a generous dollop of whipped cream in the centre. Stirring steadily, I mentally prepared myself for my first sip of chocolate – real hot chocolate.

There's no way of describing what happened next other than to say my life was set on a new course. I was in love with Paris, in love with chocolate, and in love with spending time alone discovering the world in all of its sensory delight. It was right there over my first cup of *chocolat chaud* that I vowed to one day create my own patisserie so enchanting and iconic that people would have that same sensory discovery when biting into one of my creations. It was just a matter of time before it would all fall into place.

SAUCES, FILLINGS & FROSTINGS

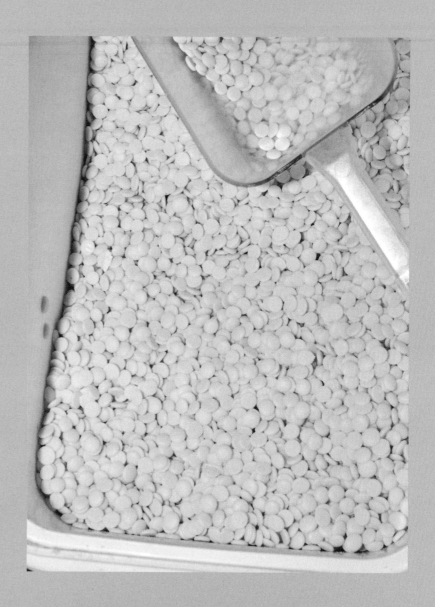

We've reached the part of the cookbook where you'll find all the extra bits and bobs that will add that 'something extra' to your next baking session. Recipes for these delicious sauces, curds, fillings and frostings can not only be followed for the bakes that require them in this book, but they can also be used to create your own spin by mixing and matching your favourite flavours. I like to think of cookbooks as a starting point for your own adventures in the kitchen, so don't shy away from letting your creativity run wild when pairing these luxurious add-ons with your next baking creation!

Brooki's Buttercream

In the bakery, I am mostly on the cake decorating station. I find a lot of joy in stacking, crumb coating and decorating cakes, which is probably due to my Virgo perfectionist nature. If there's one recipe I have made more than any other, it would be my buttercream. I have tried many buttercream styles and recipes over the years, but this is my favourite for a glossy buttercream that coats cakes perfectly.

PREPARATION TIME: 15 MINUTES

500 g (1 lb 1oz) unsalted butter, room temperature
340 g (12 oz) icing sugar, sifted
1 teaspoon of vanilla extract

In the bowl of a stand mixer with the paddle attachment, beat the butter on medium-high speed for 5 minutes. Scrape down the sides of the bowl as required.

With the mixer on low, add the sifted icing sugar. Once incorporated, increase the speed to high and beat for a further 5–8 minutes until light and fluffy.

Add the vanilla on low speed, until just incorporated.

STORAGE
Store this buttercream in the fridge in an airtight container for up to 7 days.

Chocolate Buttercream

When it comes to buttercream, the only limit to the different types you can make is your imagination. But sometimes, keeping it simple is best, especially when it comes to classic flavours, like chocolate.

There's no better way to sandwich together layers of chocolate cake than with a gloriously rich chocolate buttercream.

PREPARATION TIME: 20 MINUTES

450 g (1 lb) unsalted butter, room temperature
50 ml (2½ tablespoons) full cream milk
340 g (12 oz) dark chocolate, broken into pieces
1½ tablespoons of vanilla extract
400 g (14 oz) icing sugar, sifted

In the microwave, heat the chocolate in 15-second intervals until just melted. Be careful not to overheat the chocolate.

Alternatively, you can melt the chocolate over medium-high heat in a bowl over a saucepan of gently simmering water until liquid.

In the bowl of a stand mixer with the paddle attachment, beat butter on medium-high speed until smooth and pale in colour, about 5 minutes. Add milk and vanilla, beating until combined.

Add icing sugar on low speed and beat until creamy. On low speed, pour in melted chocolate. Mix until completely combined, glossy and smooth.

STORAGE
Store in the fridge in an airtight container for up to 7 days. It's easiest to work with when brought back up to room temperature.

Swiss Meringue Buttercream

There are many different buttercream recipes to try on your baking journey and, although a little more complex than others, a Swiss meringue buttercream is essential to master. This type of buttercream is glossy and silky and melts in the mouth with every bite, which makes it a great choice for filling macarons or topping cupcakes, so that your bite-sized bakes are big in flavour.

PREPARATION TIME: 30 MINUTES

7 large egg whites, room temperature
400 g (14 oz) caster sugar
340 g (12 oz) unsalted butter, room temperature
2 teaspoons of vanilla extract
pinch of salt

Make sure the bowl of your stand mixer is completely grease free, as this recipe will not work if there's any fat residue on the bowl or the whisk.

Place the egg whites and sugar in a heatproof bowl and use electric handheld beaters to whisk until combined. Place over a saucepan filled with a few centimetres of simmering water to create a bain-marie, ensuring the bowl is not touching the water.

Whisk the egg whites and sugar continuously until the sugar has dissolved, about 4 minutes. The mixture will thin out and become frothy on top. To test it is ready, you can use a sugar thermometer – it should be 71°C (160°F).

Immediately transfer the mixture to the bowl of a stand mixer with the whisk attachment. Beat the mixture on medium-high speed until stiff peaks form, around 10–15 minutes.

Change the whisk attachment for the paddle attachment. On medium-high speed, add 1 tablespoon of butter at a time. Wait for the butter to be completely combined before adding the next tablespoon. When all the butter has been added, turn the mixer down to medium speed and add the vanilla and salt. Mix until incorporated.

STORAGE
Store at room temperature in an airtight container for 1–2 days, or in the fridge for up to 5 days.

Mock Swiss Meringue Buttercream

If you crave the silky-smooth consistency of a Swiss meringue buttercream but need a simpler version, this no-cook adaptation is a great alternative (and an easy one to have in your recipe repertoire).

PREPARATION TIME: 20 MINUTES

1 tablespoon of meringue powder
225 g (8 oz) icing sugar
45 ml (1¾ fl oz) water
450 g (1 lb) unsalted butter, room temperature
1 teaspoon of vanilla extract

In the bowl of a stand mixer with a whisk attachment, whisk the meringue powder, icing sugar and water on medium-high speed to make royal icing.

Add the butter and vanilla, and beat until silky smooth, about 12 minutes.

STORAGE
Store in an airtight container in the fridge for up to 7 days.

Cream Cheese Frosting

My love for cream cheese frosting knows no bounds, and it is perhaps unsurprising that my favourite sponge cakes are almost always smothered in the stuff, no matter what kind they are. With its full-fat flavour and rich, moreish texture, how could cream cheese not be one of my favourite ingredients in the kitchen? This Cream Cheese Frosting is made and used in the bakery daily as the supporting act to some of our bestselling bakes, such as Red Velvet Cupcakes, Hummingbird Cupcakes and Cinnamon Scroll Cookies. The trick to finding the perfect use for a cream cheese frosting is to start with a more balanced base note (like the mild acidity of red velvet, which utilises vinegar to react with Dutch cocoa powder), so that the cream cheese frosting acts to amplify the existing qualities and provide necessary sweetness.

PREPARATION TIME: 10 MINUTES
CHILLING TIME: 2 HOURS

450 g (1 lb) Philadelphia cream cheese, room temperature and cubed
200 g (7 oz) unsalted butter, room temperature
1½ teaspoons of vanilla extract
600 g (1lb 5 oz) icing sugar, sifted

In the bowl of a stand mixer with the paddle attachment, beat the cream cheese and butter on medium speed until smooth, about 3 minutes.

Add the vanilla and beat well. Gradually add the icing sugar on low speed until fully incorporated, before increasing to high speed. Continue to beat on high speed until smooth and creamy, about 5 minutes.

Refrigerate for 2 hours to thicken before using.

STORAGE
Store in an airtight container in the fridge for up to 7 days.

Chocolate Ganache

Having a chocolate ganache recipe in your arsenal is essential for baking. This recipe is so easy, you'll likely learn it by heart. The 1:1 mixture of thickened cream and high-quality chocolate is melted until it is silky smooth and glossy, and acts to heighten your chocolate-based creations with a delicious moreishness.

PREPARATION TIME: 10 MINUTES

250 g (9 oz) milk or dark chocolate, broken into pieces
250 ml (8 fl oz) thickened cream

Place the chocolate in a heatproof bowl.

Place cream in a microwave-safe bowl and microwave for 15 -second intervals until it just begins to bubble (about 90 seconds). Alternatively, you can heat the cream over medium-high heat in a saucepan until the chocolate is completely melted and glossy in appearance.

Pour the hot cream over the chocolate and allow to sit for 2 minutes before stirring to combine.

STORAGE
Store in an airtight container in the fridge for up to 1 week or in the freezer for up to 3 months.

Lemon Curd

Nothing beats homemade lemon curd, especially in the summer months when freshness and piquancy are what's called for. Whether I'm filling lemon tarts or drizzling fresh lemon curd over a home-baked pavlova, I love having a jar at the ready.

MAKES: 450 G (1 LB)
PREPARATION TIME: 10 MINUTES
CHILLING TIME: 2 HOURS

2 eggs + 2 egg yolks, room temperature
115 g (4 oz) caster sugar
80 g (2¾ oz) unsalted butter, room temperature and cubed
zest and juice of 2 lemons

Whisk the whole eggs, yolks and caster sugar in a saucepan until smooth. Place over medium heat and add the butter, zest and juice. Whisk continuously until thickened.

Strain through a sieve into a glass jar and allow to cool before storing in the fridge.

STORAGE
Store in the fridge for up to 2 weeks, or in the freezer for up to 1 month.

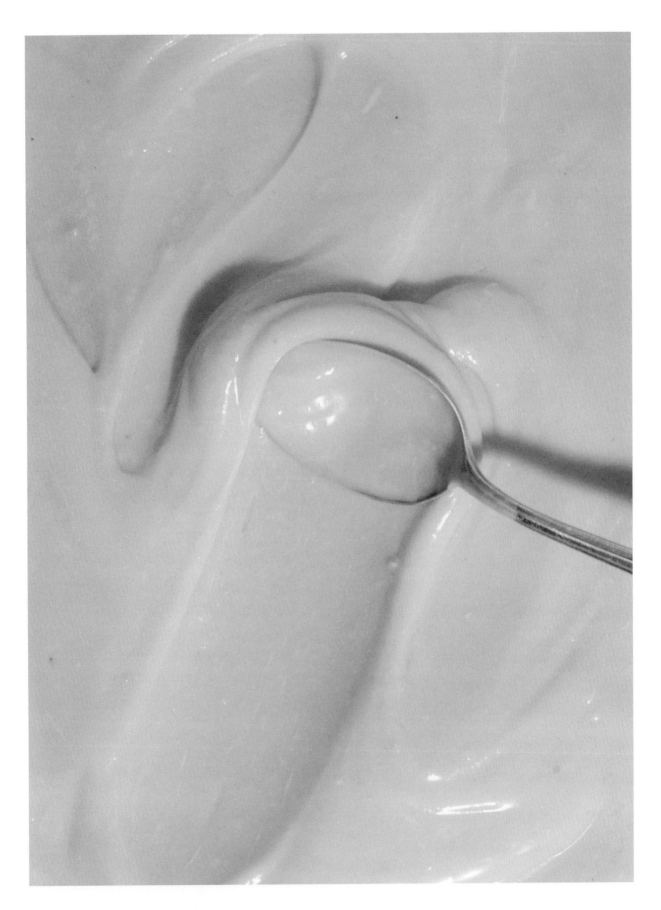

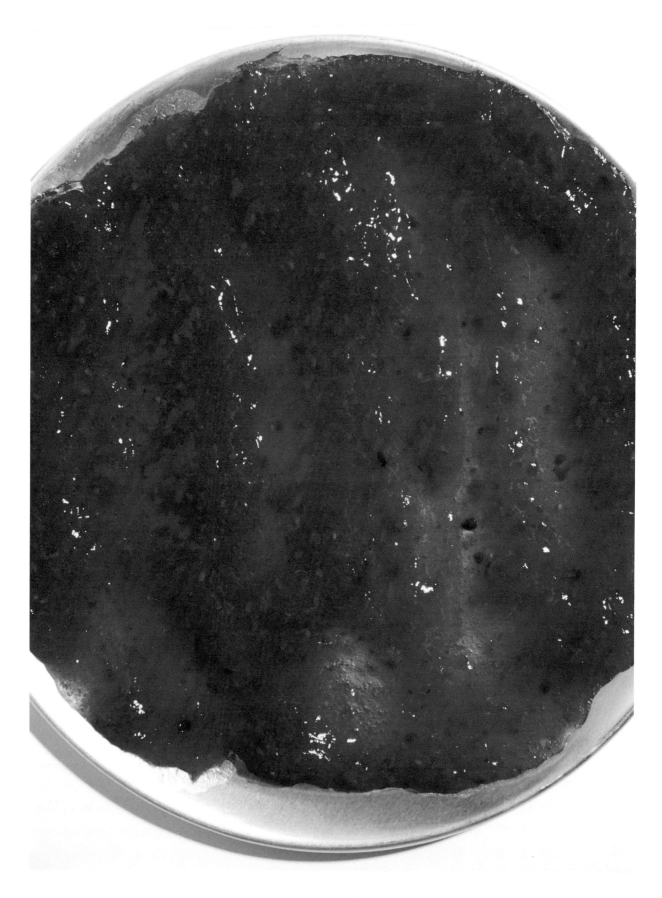

Raspberry Coulis

While it might have a fancy French name, every type of coulis is ridiculously easy to make. The name itself translates to 'flowing' or 'running', which is essentially what you will create when you combine berries and sugar, melt them over high heat and strain until you have a smooth sauce – or a coulis.

MAKES: 450 G (1 LB)
PREPARATION TIME: 5 MINUTES
CHILLING TIME: 2 HOURS

350 g (12¼ oz) fresh raspberries
100 g (3½ oz) caster sugar
4 tablespoons of water
pinch of salt

Place all ingredients in a saucepan over medium-high heat, bring to the boil and simmer until sugar has dissolved.

Transfer to a blender or use a stick blender to puree until smooth.

Using a mesh sieve, strain mixture into a bowl and discard seeds.

Refrigerate for at least 2 hours before serving.

STORAGE
Store in an airtight container in the fridge for up to 1 week.

Berry Compote

Simple to make and offering an easy way to amplify summer bakes, berry compote is one of my favourite things to make throughout the warmer months.

This Berry Compote is quick and easy to cook, and can be made with fresh or frozen berries, depending on what you have to hand.

MAKES: 300 G (10 ½ OZ)
PREPARATION TIME: 10 MINUTES

300 g (10½ oz) mixed berries (fresh or frozen)
juice of ½ a lemon
1 tablespoon of caster sugar

In a medium saucepan, heat the berries and lemon juice over medium-high heat for 3–4 minutes.

Bring to the boil, then reduce the heat slightly and cook for a few more minutes.

Add the sugar and stir well, then add more lemon juice to taste (you can adjust how much you add depending on how sweet you want the compote).

Remove from the heat and either serve warm or allow to cool and chill in the fridge to use later.

STORAGE
Store in an airtight container in the fridge for up to 2 weeks.

Crème Anglaise

Also affectionately known as custard in Australia, a crème anglaise recipe is always useful to have on hand, as it brings a luxuriously smooth texture and intense aroma of vanilla to your favourite puddings and desserts, such as Sticky Date Pudding (page 229) and Apple Crumble (page 234).

In winter, when hot desserts are on my weekly rotation, having a stash of crème anglaise handy in the fridge to reheat at any time serves as a bonus addition to wow guests, or just takes my weeknights watching rom-coms to another level.

SERVES: 4
PREPARATION TIME: 15 MINUTES
COOKING TIME: 10 MINUTES

225 ml (7½ fl oz) thickened cream
340 ml (11½ fl oz) full cream milk
120 g (4¼ oz) caster sugar
1 vanilla pod
6 egg yolks

In a medium saucepan, heat the cream, milk and half the sugar over medium heat. Use a sharp knife to split the vanilla pod lengthways without cutting all the way through, then scrape the seeds into the milk. Mix continuously with a whisk until the mixture bubbles around the edges, about 2 minutes. Remove from the heat and allow the mixture to stand for 20 minutes.

Meanwhile, whisk the egg yolks with the remaining sugar in a large bowl.

Pour a small amount of the hot cream mixture into the egg yolk mixture, whisking vigorously while you pour. Add another small amount of the hot cream and whisk again, to temper the eggs and prevent them from scrambling.

Pour this egg yolk mixture into the saucepan of cream and return to a medium heat.

Continue to stir until the custard has thickened enough to coat the back of a spoon, about 5–7 minutes.

Remove from the heat and cool in an ice bath to stop the custard from cooking, or place in the fridge with plastic wrap touching the surface to ensure a skin does not form.

STORAGE
Store in an airtight container in the fridge for up to 5 days.

BROOKI'S TIP
An ice bath is used to quickly cool foods directly after cooking. To prepare an ice bath, fill a large bowl with ice and cold water shortly before you'll need it, ensuring that the bowl is large enough for the saucepan to nest in comfortably without ice cubes getting jammed between the two vessels.

Hot Chocolate Fudge Sauce

I'm not even going to try to hide the fact that I have to finish every evening meal off with something sweet (by this point, I'm sure it's a surprise to a total of no-one). Some nights, when I'm too lazy to pull something together, I just grab some vanilla ice-cream and pour this Hot Chocolate Fudge Sauce on top. You can make it in advance and heat it up in the microwave for similarly sweet emergencies.

MAKES: 400 ML (13 ½ FL OZ)
PREPARATION TIME: 5 MINUTES

60 g (2 oz) Dutch cocoa powder
240 g (5½ oz) caster sugar
125 ml (4 fl oz) cold water
1 teaspoon of vanilla extract

In a small saucepan, whisk together the cocoa and sugar. Add the water and bring to a boil over medium heat.

Reduce to a simmer and heat for a few minutes, stirring constantly.

Remove from the heat and stir in the vanilla.

STORAGE
Store in the fridge for up to 2 weeks and reheat in the microwave as you need.

Salted Caramel Sauce

I've lost count of how many times I have made this Salted Caramel Sauce, because I've been making it in big batches in the bakery and at home almost every other week for years! This is my favourite sauce to have on hand and you'll almost always find a jar on the top shelf in my fridge. I often heat it up to pour over ice-cream late in the evenings, use it in cake fillings, or just grab a spoon and enjoy a mouthful when I'm craving something sweet. Yes, it really is that good!

MAKES: 450 ML (15 FL OZ)
PREPARATION TIME: 10 MINUTES

240 g (8 ½ oz) caster sugar
90 g (3 oz) unsalted butter, cubed and chilled
120 ml (4 fl oz) thickened cream
1 teaspoon of salt

Heat sugar in a medium saucepan over medium heat, stirring continuously with a heat-resistant spatula. Sugar clumps will form but eventually melt as you continue to stir.

Once the sugar has melted, carefully stir in the butter, one cube at a time, until melted and combined. Be careful, as the caramel will be hot and you don't want the butter to splash.

Once the butter has melted (around 1 minute), slowly pour in the cream against the side of the saucepan. Be careful, as the caramel will steam as you do this.

Allow the caramel to bubble for another minute, stirring continuously.

Remove from the heat, add salt and stir. Allow the caramel to cool before placing in a glass jar to store in the fridge or enjoying on top of your favourite dessert.

STORAGE
Store in an airtight container for up to 1 month.

Butterscotch Sauce

This Butterscotch Sauce recipe is simple and relatively quick to pull together. I love watching it deepening in colour as it intensifies in flavour while simmering over a low heat. The trick to a quality butterscotch sauce is to use a high-fat butter for a full-bodied depth, which is made even more delicious with the addition of thickened cream and, of course, brown sugar for the signature sweet caramel character.

MAKES: 600 ML (20 FL OZ)
PREPARATION TIME: 10 MINUTES

115 g (4 oz) unsalted butter
330 g (11½ oz) brown sugar
½ teaspoon of salt
240 ml (8 fl oz) thickened cream
1 tablespoon of vanilla extract

In a medium saucepan, melt the butter, brown sugar and salt over medium heat, stirring to combine.

Bring to a boil then reduce the heat slightly, continuing to stir for a further 2–3 minutes.

Lower the heat to a simmer and slowly pour in the cream. Bring to a gentle simmer for a further 4–5 minutes, stirring often.

Finally, add the vanilla and stir to combine.

Remove from the heat and allow to cool before serving or storing. The sauce will thicken as it stands.

STORAGE
Store for up to 2 weeks in the fridge in a glass jar.

FOOD
WASH
ONLY

ACKNOWLEDGEMENTS

The most important thank you goes to my publisher, Izzy, at Penguin Random House Australia, who believed in me enough to bring this cookbook to life. As a baker, you never think your dream of publishing a cookbook will actually become reality, so for both giving me the opportunity and believing that I could put this together in the busiest period of my life – I am so grateful to Izzy. To everyone who works at Penguin Random House Australia and publishing houses the world over, for keeping the publishing dream alive, thank you! I have never, nor will I ever, stop buying books; there is something so irreplaceable about the memories they hold, especially in the kitchen.

To my team at Brooki, who work tirelessly every day to meet the gruelling demands of operating a bakery. Every single person who has joined the team is part of the reason we are where we are today, and without you, none of this would be possible. Managing a team is a bit like conducting an orchestra – without each of the musicians playing their part, there is no symphony.

To my husband, Justice, who is my self-proclaimed number-one fan. Thank you for documenting every step of my bakery journey with your behind-the-scenes iPhone photos – often blurry and unflattering but always done with a sparkle in your eye. I would not be half as happy in this lifetime without your constant kindness, humility and unfaltering patience. I have never known love or joy like I do now in every aspect of my life, because you're in it.

To my extended support network – I won the lottery with my family and friends alike. Every endeavour I undertake is done with your smiling faces and cheers of support in mind – I can see and hear them now! Thanks to my mum for sharing so many of these recipes with me through my childhood and paving the way for me to create my own. And thanks to my dad for being the ever-energetic taste tester, encouraging us along in the kitchen for your gain and ours!

To every single aspiring baker out there who has ever watched a video, commented, or sent me a DM, email or letter in the post – this cookbook is for you and because of you. Please know your support means more to me than words can express and there will forever be a place in my heart for each and every one of you.

INDEX

CONVERSION CHART

The difference between measuring cups and spoons varies slightly from country to country. All cup and spoon measurements are level. One North American measuring cup holds 240 ml. One Australian metric measuring cup holds 250 ml, one Australian metric tablespoon holds 20 ml and one Australian teaspoon holds 5 ml. North America, New Zealand and the United Kingdom use a 15 ml tablespoon. Oven temperatures in this book are for fan-forced ovens. If you use a conventional oven, increase the temperature by 10–20°C.

DRY MEASUREMENTS

metric g	imperial oz		
15 g	½ oz	250 g	9 oz
20 g	¾ oz	265 g	9¼ oz
30g	1 oz	270 g	9½ oz
35 g	1¼ oz	285 g	10 oz
40 g	1½ oz	290 g	10¼ oz
50 g	1¾ oz	300 g	10½ oz
60 g	2 oz	320 g	11¼ oz
65 g	2¼ oz	325 g	11½ oz
70 g	2½ oz	340 g	12 oz
80 g	2¾ oz	345 g	12 oz
85 g	3 oz	350 g	12¼ oz
90g	3 oz	360 g	12¾ oz
100 g	3½ oz	365 g	13 oz
110 g	3¾ oz	395 g	14 oz
115 g	4 oz	400 g	14 oz
125 g	4½ oz	420 g	15 oz
140 g	5 oz	450 g	1 lb)
150 g	5¼ oz	500 g	1 lb 1oz
155 g	5½ oz	545 g	1 lb 3 oz
160 g	5½ oz	550 g	1 lb 3 oz
165 g	5¾ oz	560 g	1lb 3¾ oz
170 g	6 oz	600 g	1lb 5 oz
180g	6¼ oz	630 g	1 lb 6 oz
185	6½ oz	690 g	1 lb 8 oz
190 g	6¾ oz	700 g	1lb 8½ oz
200 g	7 oz	840 g	1 lb 13 oz
225 g	8 oz	1 kg	2 lb 3 oz
240 g	8½ oz		

LIQUID MEASUREMENTS

metric (ml)	imperial (fl oz)	Australian cup
55 ml	2 fl oz	¼ cup
75 ml	2½ fl oz	
80 ml	3 fl oz	1/3 cup
110 ml	3¾ fl oz	
125 ml	4 fl oz	½ cup
150 ml	5 fl oz	
160 ml	5½ fl oz	
175 ml	5¾ fl oz	¾ cup
180 ml	6 fl oz	
200 ml	6½ fl oz	
225 ml	7½ fl oz	
250 ml	8 fl oz	1 cup
270 ml	9½ fl oz	
300 ml	10 fl oz	1¼ cups
340 ml	11½ fl oz	1½ cups
360 ml	12 fl oz	
380 ml	13 fl oz	1⅔ cups
400 ml	13½ fl oz	1¾ cups
480 ml	1 pint	
500 ml	17 fl oz	2 cups
540 ml	18¼ fl oz	

OVEN TEMPERATURES

°C fan-forced	°F
100°	250°
110°	260°
130°	300°
140°	325°
160°	350°
170°	375°
180°	400°
200°	425°
210°	450°

PENGUIN BOOKS

UK | USA | Canada | Ireland | Australia
India | New Zealand | South Africa | China

Penguin Books is part of the Penguin Random House group of companies
whose addresses can be found at global.penguinrandomhouse.com.

Penguin
Random House
Australia

First published by Penguin Books, 2024

Cover and internal design by Andy Warren Design © Penguin Random House Australia
Typeset in TT Fors and ITC Souvenir by Post Pre-press Group, Australia

Printed and bound in China

A catalogue record for this
book is available from the
National Library of Australia

ISBN 978 1 76134 633 0

penguin.com.au

*We at Penguin Random House Australia acknowledge that Aboriginal and
Torres Strait Islander peoples are the first storytellers and Traditional Custodians
of the land on which we live and work. We honour Aboriginal and Torres Strait
Islander peoples' continuous connection to Country, waters, skies and
communities. We celebrate Aboriginal and Torres Strait Islander stories, traditions
and living cultures; and we pay our respects to Elders past and present.*